To Jeffrey + Nicola —

   With love + appreciation
for your ongoing support of
the Chabad House, and
of our friendship!

   Rabbi Gershon + Sara Leah
      Overlander

   Happy Chanukah!

D1809609

Vedibarta Bam

And You Shall Speak of Them

A compilation of selected
Torah insights, thought-provoking ideas,
homilies and explanations on

Chanukah

by

Rabbi Moshe Bogomilsky

5765 • 2005

VEDIBARTA BAM—AND YOU SHALL SPEAK OF THEM
CHANUKAH

Published and Copyrighted © by
Rabbi Moshe Bogomilsky
1382 President Street
Brooklyn, New York 11213

First Impression — 5763 • 2002
Second Impression — 5765 • 2005

ISBN 1-8808-8071-7

This *Sefer* is lovingly dedicated in honor of my wife
Randi – רבקה פריידל
and my children
Elizabeth Jewel – ליבא חיה
and
Jacqueline Paige – שרה צירל רחל

In the *Al Hanisim* prayer recited on *Chanukah* in the *Tefillot* and *Birkat Hamazon*, we recall the threat to our spiritual existence and Hashem's salvations. The introduction is "In the days of Matityahu the Hasmonai *ubanav* — and his sons (children)." It concludes with "Thereafter, Your *children* came to Your holy Temple, kindled the lights in the Courtyards of Your Sanctuary, and they established these eight days of *Chanukah* to express thanks and praise to Your great Name."

This great festival of lights — *Chanukah* celebrates the family. The seven-branched *Menorah*, made of one piece, symbolizes the completeness of the Jewish family. Seven are the immediate family members — father, mother, son, daughter, brother, sister and spouse. Cherish these relationships, as they are our most special and valuable possessions.

Always remember the lesson of the *Menorah*. Moshe is building the Tabernacle, the *Mishkan*, Hashem's earthly abode. The time arrives for the construction of the *Menorah* — the mystical symbol of wisdom that will illuminate the inner sanctum. The construction of this vessel is exceedingly complicated, and to make matters even more difficult, the entire *Menorah* is to be made from a single ingot of gold. To make the construction easier, G-d reveals the blueprints of the *Menorah* in a vision. Although Moshe gives it his best effort, he cannot accomplish this baffling task. Finally, Hashem instructs Moshe to throw the gold into the fire, and the *Menorah* will emerge by itself. And, this is exactly what happens.

There is a tremendous power inherent in the human will. When a person's heart is set on a goal and consumed with a flaming desire to attain that goal, nothing can stand in the way. This is what Hashem was teaching Moshe — nothing stands in the way of the indomitable human will, not even the mere impossibility of forming the intricate *Menorah* from a single piece of gold. The fire of his enthusiasm would create the *Menorah,* even if his hands could not. One must have a vision and dream, whether or not the dream can become a reality.

King Solomon — the wisest of all men, said, "The soul of man is a candle of G-d" (*Mishlei* 20:27). In every person is a *Menorah* — a lamp of G-d. Most wait for someone to light it — but in the case of leaders, they not only light their own souls, but the souls of others, and radiate that light throughout the community. G-d doesn't need our help in spreading light — He can light all the lights alone, but He wants us to be involved in the lighting. Every one of us has the opportunity to share and to grow brighter along with others. By commanding us to light the *Menorah,* G-d gives us not merely a place under the lights — He gives us the opportunity to radiate on our own, and to help others to shine as well. This is the example that I have tried to set for you.

When the Rabbis of the generation decided that the miracle of *Chanukah* be commemorated through candle lighting, they ordained that *neir ish ubeito* — a candle for a man and his household (*Shabbat* 21b). According to the *Gemara* (*Yoma* 12a) *beito* refers to *ishto,* ones wife.

> *"Wealth and Riches are in his house*
> *and his charity endures forever."*
> TEHILLIM 112:3

Randi, thank you for making my life so complete and filling our home with wealth and riches — Elizabeth Jewel and Jacqueline Paige.

I pray that Hashem bless you and our entire family with good health and longevity to see our young candles, Elizabeth and Jacqueline, grow to be luminaries in the Jewish community.

Arthur Luxenberg

Chanukah, 5763

TABLE OF CONTENTS

FOREWORD

As mentioned in some of the other *seforim* in the *Vedibarta Bam* series it was never my ambition to be a publisher nor was I trained to be a writer. The purpose of the *seforim* I printed until now and will, please G-d, publish, is to provide a medium which will unite our family, past, present and future.

When Yehudah pleaded with Yosef to release Binyamin, he stressed the bond between Binyamin and Yaakov by saying *"venafsho keshurah benafsho"* — "and his soul is bound up with his soul" (*Bereishit* 44:30). The word *"keshurah"* (קשורה) in Torah numerology adds up to 611, as does the word "Torah." Yehudah's message was that the relationship of Yaakov and his children was not just biological but that they were soul-mates. This unique bond was created by the Torah Yaakov conveyed to his children, and similarly Torah is the language which unites the Jewish people of all generations.

Towards that end I publish these *seforim* and pray that they be used by my children, grandchildren and future generations. Words cannot adequately describe how gratifying it is to hear one of our young grandchildren say *"Zeide,* I read it in your *sefer."*

On *Chanukah* we celebrate our victory over the Syrian-Greeks, whose goal was *"lehashkicham Toratechah"* — to stop the Jewish people from studying Torah and make them ultimately forget it. The best way to celebrate such a victory is through engaging in the study of Torah. This is also why the emphasis of *Chanukah* is the kindling of the *Menorah,* since candles and light are analogous to Torah and *mitzvot.* As King

Shlomo says, "For a *mitzvah* is candle and Torah is light" (Proverbs 6:23).

When the sages instituted the kindling of the *Menorah* on *Chanukah*, they ordained that it be *"neir ish ubeito"* — a candle for a man and his family. More than on any other *Yom Tov*, the emphasis here is on family and household. And most probably this may also be an explanation for all the family gatherings that commonly take place during *Chanukah*.

As is customary, our family too would arrange a *Chanukah* party for the entire family. It was a chance for me to meet my uncles, aunts and cousins. And in more recent years, after my wife and I married and had a family of our own, it gave our children an opportunity to meet their cousins and great uncles and aunts. The highlight was when my grandfather Rabbi Tzvi *Hakohen* Kaplan ע״ה would deliver his address and message. Even my children, some of who are amongst the oldest grandchildren may remember my mother, *Buby* Hadassah's ע״ה *rogelach,* which were a favorite, but they are too young to remember my grandfather and especially not his *dvar Torah*.

Almost every year he would say something similar, and in another part of this book, I printed it under the caption "My *Ziede's Chanukah* Message." The gist of his message was that his and my grandmother *Buby* Yehudis' wish is that their children and grandchildren conduct homes in the spirit of authentic Torah teaching. Their greatest desire was that their offspring not just be *shomrei* Torah and *mitzvot* but also *lomdei* Torah, ones who set aside time for Torah study.

Let the following suffice to portray the love for Torah he possessed and transmitted to his children. My grandfather was an exceptional *Talmid Chacham*. According to my uncle, Reb Shimon *Hakohen* Kaplan, his admittance to the very prominent Yeshivah of Mir prior to his *bar mitzvah* made him the youngest student every accepted there. After his marriage, he settled in the city of Mir, where he taught in the *yeshivah ketana* of the Mirer Yeshivah.

My grandparents arrived in the United States, together with their five children on November 18, 1924. Soon thereafter, my grandfather joined the faculty of Yeshivah Torah Vodaat where he taught Torah to many students over his 27 year tenure. My mother, the oldest of the children, was 12 years old. There were no *frum* schools for girls so she attended a public elementary and high school in Brooklyn, New York. Her Torah education she received at home under the tutelage of her parents.

In the 1930's when marriage became a subject, my grandfather wrote to Rabbi Yeruchem Levovitz ע״ה, the *Mashgiach* at Mir Yeshivah in Poland, asking whether he had a Torah scholar of high caliber suitable as a prospect for marriage for his daughter, my mother. After Reb Yeruchem's positive reply, my mother traveled to Mir, all alone, and my parents' wedding took place in the neighboring town of Steipz.

She then came back to the United States with my father, Rabbi Shmuel Pesach Bogomilsky ע״ה, and he assumed a position as a *Rav* in Bronx, New York, where he quickly became renowned as a great *Talmid Chacham*. Unfortunately, this period of fame was all-too-brief: he expired while delivering a *derashah* a few years later.

My mother remained widowed for almost a decade and would only consider marriage to a *talmid chacham,* since it would benefit myself and my brother Rabbi Shmuel Pesach שי׳ Bogomilsky. Her wish was realized when she married Rabbi Eli Moshe Liss ע״ה who for many years served as a *mashpia* at the Lubavitcher Yeshivah in Brooklyn, New York and our connection with Lubavitch is thanks to him.

Times have, thank G-d, changed in the United States but our desires remained the same as our parents and grandparents. It is our fervent wish that our children raise their families in the spirit of Torah and *Chassidut* and that they be a source of *Yiddish* and *Chassidish nachas* to us.

If it were up to me and my wife Bracha, we would make a *Chanukah* party and invite our children and grandchildren, but unfortunately that is not feasible, since they are living in different states and some grandchildren are studying in out-of-town *yeshivot* or abroad. Therefore, when our children and grandchildren will all read and study this *Vedibarta Bam* on *Chanukah*, we hope they will reflect on their parents and grandparents, Bracha and Moshe, alluded to in the word *Bam*. May the Torah spoken in this book unite us all so that we will enjoy an inspiring and luminous *Chanukah*.

In this book there is considerable discussion of the connection between *Chanukah* and *Mashiach*. In fact, in the *sefer*, *Ma'or Einayim*, of the Chassidic Rebbe, Reb Mordechai זצ״ל of Chernobyl, it is explained that King David's statement "*Arachti neir limeshichai*" — "I have prepared a candle for my anointed" (Psalms 132:17) means that *Chanukah* is a preparation for the revelation of *Mashiach*, and when we light the candles we are treated to a semblance of the great light that we will enjoy in those days. Let us hope that this will be realized speedily in our times. Moreover, when *Mashiach* arrives, may we be able to proudly present our dear family to him.

ABOUT THE *SEFER*

In the entire Babylonian Talmud *Chanukah* is mentioned only a few times in *Mishnah* and discussed over a few pages of *Gemara* in the tractate of *Shabbat*. Nevertheless, it has earned itself a venerable spot in Talmudic, halachic, homiletic and Chassidic literature.

Many *sefarim* have been written which expound the Halachic details and miracles of the *Yom Tov*. Multitudes of chapters have been written in countless *sefarim* which elaborate on the significance of the *Yom Tov* and its practical implications in one's life. In the works of the great Chassidic leaders too, *Chanukah* holds a very prominent place and many of them see *Chanukah* as the link and preparation to the most glorious and eagerly anticipated revelation of *Mashiach* and the Messianic Era.

To capsulize everything in one *sefer* is an impossibility, but it was my endeavor to present this *sefer* as a comprehensive anthology on *Chanukah*. In it the reader will find halachic observations, homeletic interpretations, insights on the miracles, and practical implications which can be derived for our daily life from this luminous eight-day celebration. In addition, included is also an English translation of *Megilat Antiochus* — The Scroll of the Hasmoneans, which is read in some synagogues on *Chanukah,* and contains some enlightening history of that period.

Since the *Chanukah* lights commemorate the kindling of the Holy *Menorah* of the *Beit Hamikdash,* a special section has been added on the *Menorah* and its oil to discuss in detail how and where in the *Beit Hamikdash* it was placed and kindled. We also provided insights that can be derived from some of the Torah's commands regarding the making of the *Menorah* itself and the oil used for its kindling.

In keeping with the style of all the previous *sefarim* in the *Vedibarta Bam* series, the thoughts have been presented in a question and answer form. This method has received acclaim since it enhances the reader's comprehension and challenges his or her thinking.

ACKNOWLEDGMENTS

A *sefer* cannot be produced single-handedly. The cooperation, input and assistance of many is a prerequisite. To make it a reality, a minimum of a writer, editor, secretary, graphic designer, publisher and distributor are necessary. Our team consisted of all of these and some played more than one role.

In retrospect, the reward for most valuable player on our team goes to Yitzchok Turner, In addition to his skill in the art of layout and typography which makes this *sefer* aesthetically attractive, he served as the secretary who painstakingly copied the entire *sefer* from my not-easily-readable hand-written notes. Were it not for his unlimited patience and refined character, he undoubtedly would have stopped copying even before finishing the first page.

Thank G-d, the *Vedibarta Bam* series has entered into many homes of all Jewish circles and is used and studied considerably. Besides my expressing appreciation, may the *zechut* for *Talmud Torah* he propagated through his efforts be a source of eternal blessing for him and his family.

Rabbi Yonah Avtzon has made it his goal in life to disseminate the Lubavitcher Rebbe's teachings, through his organization Sichot In English. His success in this endeavor is impressive and enviable.

I thank him most profusely for making available to me his facilities and for his dedicated efforts in bringing my books to all facets of the Jewish community in United States and abroad.

My editor, Dr. Binyamin Kaplan has been working with me since the first volume of this series was published. He is a genius at taking my writing and, with the stroke of his pen, making it a literary piece of work. He is now living on the West Coast and a full-time employee of the O.U. To accommodate my needs he edits my writings in the late hours of the night and the early hours of the morning. His Torah knowledge, quick grasp of a subject, and extraordinary writing skill are assets which I cherish greatly. May he and his *aishet chayil* be blessed with much success in their endeavors to raise a *chassidishe* family.

Rabbi Moshe Bogomilsky

Rosh Chodesh Kislev, 5763

12

גמרא
The Gemara's Account

גמרא

מַאי חֲנוּכָּה דְּתָנוּ רַבָּנָן בְּכ״ה בְּכִסְלֵיו יוֹמֵי דַּחֲנוּכָּה תְּמַנְיָא אִינּוּן דְּלָא לְמִסְפַּד בְּהוֹן וּדְלָא לְהִתְעַנּוֹת בְּהוֹן שֶׁכְּשֶׁנִּכְנְסוּ יְוָנִים לַהֵיכָל טִמְּאוּ כָּל הַשְּׁמָנִים שֶׁבַּהֵיכָל וּכְשֶׁגָּבְרָה מַלְכוּת בֵּית חַשְׁמוֹנַאי וְנִצְּחוּם בָּדְקוּ וְלֹא מָצְאוּ אֶלָּא פַּךְ אֶחָד שֶׁל שֶׁמֶן שֶׁהָיָה מוּנָּח בְּחוֹתָמוֹ שֶׁל כֹּהֵן גָּדוֹל וְלֹא הָיָה בּוֹ אֶלָּא לְהַדְלִיק יוֹם אֶחָד נַעֲשָׂה בּוֹ נֵס וְהִדְלִיקוּ מִמֶּנּוּ שְׁמוֹנָה יָמִים לְשָׁנָה אַחֶרֶת קְבָעוּם וַעֲשָׂאוּם יָמִים טוֹבִים בְּהַלֵּל וְהוֹדָאָה

"מַאי חֲנוּכָּה"
"Meaning of Name *Chanukah*"

QUESTION: What is the meaning of the name *"Chanukah"?*

ANSWER: 1) For a long period of time the Jews were at war with the Syrian-Greeks. Finally on the 25th of *Kislev* in the year 3597 (165 B.C.E.) the Hasmoneans vanquished the enemy, recaptured the *Beit Hamikdash,* and rested from the warfare. Thus the word *"Chanukah"* is a composite of two words: *"chanu"* — "they rested" (חנו) *"chof hei"* — "[on] the twenty fifth" of *Kislev.*

(ר״ן מס׳ שבת, ואבודרהם, ועי׳ בהשלמה לשו״ע הרב לבעל "דברי נחמיה")

2) *"Chanukah"* derives from the word *"chinuch"* — "dedication" — on this day they dedicated a new Altar. The *Gemara (Avodah Zarah 52b)* says that the Greeks defiled the Altar by using it to sacrifice offerings to an idol. The Rabbis prohibited using that Altar, and its stones were hidden away in the northeastern chamber that opened to the *Beit Hamoked* — Hall of the Fire. When the Hasmoneans seized control, they immediately built a new Altar, which was dedicated on the 25th of *Kislev.*

(מהרש״א)

Gemara

What is *Chanukah?* As the Rabbis learned, on the 25th of *Kislev* [begin] the days of *Chanukah*, eight in number, during which it is forbidden to eulogize or to fast. For when the Greeks entered the Sanctuary, they defiled all the oils that were in the Sanctuary. When the royal Hasmonean house overpowered them and vanquished them, they searched and found only one flask of oil that lay there with the *Kohen Gadol's* seal, and it contained enough oil only to kindle for one day. A miracle occurred with it, and they kindled with it for eight days. The following year [the Hasmoneans and the *Sanhedrin*] established and rendered [these eight days] as festival days — with respect to *Hallel* and "thanksgiving."

(*Shabbat* 21b)

The entire *Beit Hamikdash* needed rededication since the Syrian-Greeks defiled everything, as the *Gemara* (*Avodah Zarah* 52b) says, *"uba'u ba pritzim vayechaleluhah"* — "lawless people entered [the Sanctuary] and profaned it." Nevertheless, the *chinuch* — rededication — of the Altar is emphasized because it was targeted by the Syrian-Greeks for defilement since it represented the primary part of the *mitzvah* of erecting the *Beit Hamikdash*. As the Rambam (*Beit Habechirah* 1:1) writes, "It is a *mitzvah* to build a house for Hashem, to be prepared to be able to offer sacrifices in it."

There is a question concerning the way this dedication was accomplished. Some say that it was through doing the service on the Altar (or the using of the vessels), as the *Gemara* (*Shevuot* 15a) says, *"Avodatan mechanchatan"* — they became consecrated through their inaugural [first use in] service.

Others opine that actual rededication was not required since the *halachah* (Rambam, *Beit Habechirah* 6:14) is that the initial sanctification of *Yerushalayim* and the *Beit Hamikdash* in the days of King David and Shlomo was sufficient for that time and for all future times. Thus, even after the Babylonians destroyed *Yerushalayim* and the first *Beit Hamikdash*, the site retained its sanctity.

Therefore, in our case, *"chinuch"* does not mean formal consecration and rededication, but rather renewal of use — the putting back of the items into use again by the Jews after a long period of interruption and after the *Beit Hamikdash* was thoroughly cleaned up.

It should be noted, however, that there are opinions that the rule concerning the perpetual sanctity only applies to the *Beit Hamikdash site* and vessels which needed repair, but not to a totally newly built item, as in the case of the Altar.

(לקוטי שיחות ח״כ ע׳ 633 בהגה״ה, מועדים בהלכה)

3) There is a dispute between *Beit Shammai* and *Beit Hillel* concerning how many candles the *mehadrin min hamehadrim* — extremely scrupulous — should kindle each night. *Beit Shammai* say to kindle eight the first night and each night thereafter to decrease the number by one. *Beit Hillel* say to start with one on the first night and add another candle each succeeding night.

The word *"Chanukah"* is an acronym for *"Chet neirot vehalachah kebeit Hillel"* (ח׳ נרות והלכה כבית הלל) — "Eight candles [should be lit on *Chanukah*] and the *halachah* is like *Beit Hillel*" [to increase the number each night].

(אבודרהם והובא בעטרת זקנים על שו״ע סי׳ עת״ר או״ח)

4) In the days of *Chanukah* they miraculously kindled the *Menorah* for eight days. The *Menorah* had on it seven lamps, so during the period of the miracle they kindled seven lights for eight days, a total of 56 candles, which in Hebrew numerals is נ״ו.

Thus the name *"Chanukah"* connotes that —

ח — for eight days
נ"ו — 56 candles were miraculously kindled
כ"ה — this all started on the 25th of the month.

(בני יששכר)

5) Daryavesh (Darius) the king of Persia (according to the *Midrash* [*Vayikra Rabbah* 15:4] he was the son of Esther and Achashverosh) sanctioned and encouraged the construction of the second *Beit Hamikdash* which had begun in the days of Koresh (Cyrus, king of Persia) and which subsequently ceased for eighteen years.

The prophet Chaggai writes (2:14-18) that the *Beit Hamikdash* was completed on the 24th of the ninth month (*Kislev*). Thus, it was dedicated the next day with the offering of sacrifices, and the kindling of the *Menorah* took place in the evening, as the *Gemara* (*Menachot* 49a) states, that the dedication of the *Menorah* can only be accomplished with the evening kindling.

Consequently, because of the *chinuch* — dedication — of the *Beit Hamikdash*, which took place on this day many years earlier, the festival marking the miracle of the lights which takes place also on the 25th of *Kislev* is called "Chanukah."

(מור וקציעה מר' יעקב ז"ל עמדין סי' עת"ר – ובלקו"ש ח"כ ע' 633 כתב כ"ק אדמו"ר לא זכיתי להבין, שהרי כל השנים עד החשמונאים לא הזכירו זה)

6) The original light Hashem created was extremely powerful; one could see with it from one end of the world to the other. Reflecting upon the wickedness of man, Hashem hid it for the future, when *Mashiach* will reveal himself (*Chagigah* 12a). According to the *Midrash* (*Tanchuma, Parshat Noah* 3) it was hidden in the Torah to benefit those who toil in the Oral Torah day and night.

The Syrian-Greeks endeavored to detach Jews from Torah and wanted them to deny their belief in Hashem and *Mashiach*. When the miracle of the kindling of the *Menorah* took place, Hashem revealed a semblance of the great hidden light which will radiate in full glory in the Messianic Era.

Likewise, every *Chanukah* when the *Menorah* is kindled, there is a revelation of that great light in this mundane world.

"*Chanukah*" comes from the word "*chinuch,*" which means preparation and education. A minor is exempt from fulfilling the *mitzvot* of the Torah. Nevertheless, he goes through a process called "*chinuch*" in which he is trained and taught how to properly fulfill *mitzvot* when he will become *Bar-Mitzvah* and thereafter, for the rest of his life.

Similarly, the festival is called "*Chanukah*" because on it Hashem provides *chinuch* to the Jewish people. He prepares and educates them about the great hidden light by giving a foretaste on *Chanukah* of that illumination which they will merit to enjoy speedily in the days of *Mashiach*.

(בני יששכר)

"מאי חנוכה? בכ"ה בכסליו..."
"What is *Chanukah*? On the 25th of *Kislev*..."

QUESTION: Why did the miracle of *Chanukah* take place on the 25th of *Kislev*?

ANSWER: In the wilderness, the construction of the *Mishkan* was completed on the 25th of *Kislev*. Hashem told Moshe to wait with the dedication till the auspicious day of *Rosh Chodesh Nissan* the month in which the Patriarchs were born (*Rosh Hashanah* 11a). The 25th of *Kislev* was somewhat offended. To appease her, the rededication of the second *Beit Hamikdash,* in the days of the Hasmoneans, took place on the 25th of *Kislev*.

(ילקוט שמעוני, מלכים סוף רמז קפד, וע" לקוטי שיחות ח"י ע' 279)

* * *

It is interesting to note that the words "זאת חנוכת המזבח" (*Bamidbar* 7:84) — "this is the dedication of the Altar" — which refer to the *Mishkan* — Tabernacle — (and are part of the Torah reading for *Chanukah*), have the numerical value of 954, which is the exact numerical value of "זאת יהיה בימי

חשמונים" — "this (dedication) will be in the days of the Hasmoneans."

(רוקח)

"תנו רבנן בכ"ה בכסליו יומי דחנוכה"

"The Rabbis learned, on the 25th of *Kislev* [begin] the days of *Chanukah*."

QUESTION: Why does the *Gemara* write the name of the month, *Kislev* (כסליו) with a *yud*?

ANSWER: The word *"Kislev"* with a *yud* is an acronym for *"Vayomer Hashem salachti kidvarecha"* (ויאמר י-ה-ו-ה **סלחתי כדבריך**) — "Hashem said I have pardoned in accordance with Your words" (*Bamidbar* 14:20). This indicates that *Chanukah* is also a time for *teshuvah* and Divine forgiveness.

It is stated in *sefarim* (see *Ta'amei Haminhagim* p. 363) that *Chanukah* is the *"gemar hachatimah"* — the completion of the process (which started in *Tishrei*) by which the Jews are sealed and inscribed for the new year.

An allusion to this is found in the *pasuk* *"Bezot yechupar avon Yaakov"* — "Through this shall Yaakov's iniquity be atoned" (Isaiah 27:9). The word *"bezot"* is a reference to **Zot Chanukah,** and the prophet is saying that until *"zot"* Chanukah the sins of the Jewish people are forgiven.

Another hint is from the discussion the brothers had with their father Yaakov about returning to Egypt to purchase food. They said *"Ki lulei hitmamanu ki atah shavnu zeh pa'amayim"* — "For had we not delayed, by now we could have returned twice" (*Bereishit* 43:10). The word *"lulei"* (לולא) can be arranged to spell *"Elul"* (אלול), which is the month designated for *Teshuvah*. The message was *"Ki lulei hitmanu —* if we delayed doing *Teshuvah* in the month of *Elul, ki atah shavnu zeh pa'amayim* — we still have two more chances to do *Teshuvah* — the month of *Tishrei* and *Chanukah*."

(עי' לקו"ש חכ"ה ע' 510, אג"ק חי"ד ע' קי"ב, עיטורי תורה על בראשית)

WHY WERE THE OILS DEFILED?

"כשנכנסו יוונים להיכל טמאו כל השמנים"

"When the Greeks entered the Sanctuary they defiled all the oils."

QUESTION: If the purpose of the Greeks was to extinguish the light of the *Menorah* and prevent its rekindling, why did they *defile* the oil? They could have accomplished this more effectively by using it up or destroying it.

ANSWER: The true objective of the Greeks was not to *prevent* the rekindling of the *Menorah*, but rather that it should be rekindled with *defiled* oil. Hence, they purposely left a supply of defiled oil in the Sanctuary to be readily available for this purpose.

The Greeks were willing to recognize the Torah as a beautiful literary creation, with exceptional wisdom and profound philosophy, provided only that it was considered as a *human* creation, like their own mythology. As such, the Torah could be changed and modified from time to time, so as to harmonize with the character of the ruling class and the novel ideas and morals of the period. Thus, it was not the suppression of the Torah that they aimed at, but *"lehashkicham Toratecha"* — "to make them forget *Your* Torah" — and not treat it as G-d-given.

Similarly, they were not against to the moral and ethical values contained therein, but their concern was *"leha'aviram meichukei retzonecha"* — "to violate the decrees of *Your* Will" — not to observe the Divine *chukim*, the so-called "supra-rational" precepts, which more than any other, distinguish the Divinely ordained Jewish way of life.

Their objective was, thus, not to prevent the rekindling of the *Menorah*, but that its light should come from oil that had a Greek "taint."

(לקוטי שיחות ח"ג)

HOW WERE THE OILS DEFILED

"טמאו כל השמנים"

"They defiled all the oils that were in the Sanctuary."

QUESTION: How was the defilement caused to the flasks of oil?

ANSWER: 1) Our Rabbis decreed that the gentiles impart the *tumah* of a *zav* through *maga* — touching an item — or even by *heset* — indirectly causing an item to move. However, the unbroken seal of the *Kohen Gadol* on the flask of oil was an indication that the Syrian-Greeks did not even notice it, and it was thus ritually pure olive oil suitable for kindling the *Menorah*.

A difficulty raised with the explanation is that this law is one of the Eighteen Enactments which were established when a large contingent of disciples of Shammai and Hillel met in the upper chamber of Chananyah ben Chizkiyah ben Daron (See *Shabbat* 13b). Now the miracle of *Chanukah* took place in the year 3597, which was 206 years before the destruction of the *Beit Hamikdash* while Shammai and Hillel lived only 100 years before the destruction (*Shabbat* 15a)?

To alleviate this difficulty some say that originally gentiles were declared as *zavim* only to the extent that what they touched could not be used any more for matters of holiness, but at the time of the Eighteen Enactments the decree was extended to a point that it required that the holy things they touched needed to be destroyed by burning (see *Shabbat* 15b).

Some say that the original decree applied only to the adults and later at the time of the Eighteen Enactments it was extended to include children of nine years and older.

(רא"ם בביאוריו לסמ"ג עשין ה', ועי' פרי חדש סי' עת"ר ומהרש"א שבת כ"א ע"ב)

2) The *Gemara* (*Avodah Zarah* 52b) says that when the Greeks seized control of the *Beit Hamikdash* they defiled the

Altar by sacrificing offerings upon it to an idol. The *Gemara* (*Chullin* 13b) says that idolatrous offerings are Biblically likened to "the dead," and just as a human corpse imparts *tumah* through *ohel* — by being under the same roof — so does an idolatrous offering.

A difficulty some raise with this explanation is that this is only the opinion of Rabbi Yehudah ben Beteirah. The *Rabbanan* disagree and the *halachah* follows their opinion.

Tosafot (ibid.) says that though the *Rabbanan* do not hold that idolatrous offerings Biblically convey *Tumah* through *ohel*, they agree that a Rabbinic prohibition would apply. Accordingly, they were unable to use these oils because according to Rabbinic law they were considered *tamei*.

One can still ask, if the oil was *tamei* only from a Rabbinic standpoint, why did they not use it for kindling the *Menorah*, which is a Biblical law?

The answer is that Rabbis cannot order the active violation of a Biblical law (*kum ve'aseih*), but they have the power to stop the fulfillment of a Biblical law by *shev v'al ta'aseh* — inactivity.

3) Some say, that even if the *tumah* of *ohel* does not apply, all the flasks of oil that were open was used or may have been used for their idolatrous offerings (and afterwards poured back into the flask) and thus forbidden for our use. Since the flask found was sealed, it was definitely not used by them and therefore it was undoubtedly suitable for kindling the *Menorah*.

(אליהו רבה עת"ר סק"ג, פרי חדש, לבוש, ב"ח, חתן סופר על חנוכה סי' א')

4) In the course of the fierce fighting that took place within the *Beit Hamikdash*, numerous fatalities occurred among the Jewish soldiers. According to *halachah* the corpse of a Jew lying within the house causes everything under the same roof to become *tamei* — defiled. Hence, all the oil in the Sanctuary became *tamei* except for the one flask which had an unbroken seal on it.

Though a corpse causes everything under the same *ohel* —
roof — to become *tamei*, the flask did not become *tamei*
because the Torah (*Bamidbar* 19:15) says that an earthenware
vessel with a tightly fitting cover is not affected.

(ב״ח סי׳ עת״ר)

WHY WAS A MIRACLE NEEDED FOR EIGHT DAYS

"נעשה בו נס והדליקו ממנו שמונה ימים"

"A miracle occurred with it, and they kindled with it for eight days."

QUESTION: Why was a miracle needed for eight days?

ANSWER: 1) For the kindling of the *Menorah* not only
was the purest oil used, but also the best quality. Such oil
was manufactured in the city of Tekoa (see *Menachot* 85b),
which was in the tribal portion of Asher, who was blessed
with an abundance of oil (*Bereishit* 49:20, Rashi).

Tekoa was a four day trip from *Yerushalayim*. Thus, it
required four days to reach Tekoa and another four to return
back to *Yerushalayim*. Since all this time the single flask lasted
miraculously, it was decided to make *Chanukah* eight days in
commemoration.

(ר״ן)

A question raised about this is that in eight days there
must be a *Shabbat* and to travel out of the city more than 12
mil (a *mil* is approximately 6/10 of a mile) or to carry on
Shabbat in a public domain is a Biblical violation, so it should
have taken nine days to get new oil from Tekoa. An answer
may be that the entire eight days were not occupied with
travel; rather it was a 3 ½ day journey each way, and counting
the *Shabbat*, it would require eight days until new oil was
obtained from Tekoa.

(חתן סופר – חנוכה סי׳ ז')

2) As a result of the war the Jews became *tamei meit* —
defiled by contact with corpses — and they required seven

days of purification. An additional day was also needed to
produce the oil once the workers regained their purity.
During this entire period the flask of oil did not give out, so
an eight-day festival was declared in commemoration.

(בית יוסף אורח חיים עת"ר)

QUESTION: This raises a difficulty: If they were all *tamei*,
how were they able to kindle the *Menorah* since when they
touched the oil they would make it *tamei* and in turn it would
convey *tumah* to the *Menorah?*

ANSWER: The single sealed flask found was considered
definitely not *tamei*. When the *Kohanim* handled it to pour
into the *Menorah*, it was done through *peshutei k'lei eitz* —
simple pieces of unshaped and unformed wood which do not
attract *tumah* when touched by a *tamei meit*.

The *Gemara* (*Avodah Zarah* 43a) says that the Syrian-
Greeks plundered the golden *Menorah*, and for the time being
the Jews made a new one of wood. The new wooden *Menorah*
also was considered a *peshutei k'li eitz* and therefore did not
become *tamei* through the *tamei* craftsman who made it.

This suggests a difficulty, however: The cups containing
the oil suggest that it should not be considered a simple
wooden structure but a *k'li kibel* — receptacle — and become
tamei.

Some explain that in regard to *tumah*, a receptacle is
something that holds things for storage, and when they are
needed, the things are taken out to be used, and an example
would be a knife holder. In the *Menorah*, however, the oil was
put into the cups and then kindled; it was not put there for
storage purposes.

(בתי כהונה עפ"י תו"כ פ' שמיני פ"ו, והקשו ע"ז מתוספתא כלים, בבא מציעא פ"ב:ד)

Alternatively, the laws of *tumah* are derived from the verse
"Whether it is a wooden utensil etc. or a sack" (*Vayikra*
11:32). Since the Torah equated wood and sack, we learn that
just as a sack is an item carried laden as well as empty, so
too, must wooden utensils (or any utensil) be of a sort that is

carried laden as well as empty in order to be susceptible to *tumah*. This excludes items which must always be stationary since they are not carried either laden or empty. According to the *Gemara* (*Chagigah* 26b) the *Menorah* and the *Shulchan* — Table — are considered *"k'lei eitz ha'asu lanachat"* — "wooden utensils made to remain stationary" — and thus they do not become *tamei*.

(רא״ם, מהרש״א מס׳ שבת, תבואת שור, בתי כהונה)

"בדקו ולא מצאו אלא פך אחד
של שמן שהיה מונח בחותמו של כהן גדול"

"They searched and found only one flask of oil, that lay there with the seal of the *Kohen Gadol*."

QUESTION: What assurance did they have that the flask was not touched by any of the Greek soldiers?

ANSWER: *Tosafot* (ibid.) raises this question, and answers that it was buried in the ground, and thus the Greeks did not see it or know of its existence. A difficulty with this explanation is that there is no allusion to this fact in the *Gemara*. Moreover, if so, why was it necessary to have a seal on it?

Careful analysis of the terminology used in the *Gemara*, prompts one to ask:

1) The *Kohen Gadol* was not in charge of making oil. Why would his seal be on the flask?

2) Grammatically, instead of saying שהיה **מונח** בחותמו של כהן גדול — "that lay there with the *Kohen Gadol's* seal" — it should have said, "שהיה **חתום**" — "that was *sealed* [with the *Kohen Gadol's* seal]?"

From this we may deduce that when the Hasmoneans entered the *Beit Hamikdash*, their eyes beheld a fascinating phenomenon. They saw one flask of oil, and שהיה מונח בחותמו של כהן גדול —it was lying *together* with the precious golden signet ring of the *Kohen Gadol*. They surmised that undoubtedly no Greek had come into this area, because he definitely would have stolen the ring. Therefore, they confidently assumed that the flask was not defiled by the Greeks and fit for the *Menorah* kindling.

(צמח דוד מדינוב זצ"ל)

Why Was The Miracle of Finding Oil Necessary?

"בדקו ולא מצאו אלא פך אחד של שמן"

"They searched and found only one flask of oil."

QUESTION: There is an opinion in the *Gemara* (*Yoma* 6b) that *tumah* — defilement — is *"dechuyah betzibbur"* — overridden with regard to a community. That is, the Torah allows the needs of the communal offerings to override the *tumah* restrictions, but it does so with reluctance; it prefers that a community, too, observe *tumah* restrictions if at all possible. Another opinion holds that it is *"hutrah betzibbur"* — permitted in regard to a community. That is, if any *tumah* restriction interferes with a communal offering, Torah commands without reservation that the restriction be disregarded.

According to the latter opinion, that *tumah* is *"hutrah betzibur,"* why was the whole miracle of the oil necessary they could have used oil which was *tamei*?

ANSWER: Hashem performed this miracle, though halachically it was unnecessary, to demonstrate his love for the Jewish people, He knew that if they had no other alternative, they would reluctantly suffice with using defiled oil to kindle the *Menorah*. By giving them the opportunity to perform the *mitzvah behidur* — in the best possible way — He showed that they are His beloved people and that He wants them to be able to perform His *mitzvot* with happiness and contentment.

(חכם צבי סי' פ"ז - פני יהושע)

* * *

Alternatively, the *Gemara* (*Avodah Zarah* 43a) says that the Syrian-Greeks defiled the Sanctuary and plundered the vessels and utensils of the *Beit Hamikdash*. When the Hasmoneans were victorious and expelled the oppressors, they purified the *Beit Hamikdash* and restored the service. Since the Hasmoneans were impoverished, they were unable to make a new *Menorah* out of gold, so they made a wooden *Menorah* instead.

Now, all the utensils used in the Tabernacle and *Beit Hamikdash* service needed to be consecrated in order to achieve *kedushat haguf* — physical sanctity — making them fit for use in the *Beit Hamikdash* service. The *Gemara* (*Shevuot* 15a) says, "All the utensils that Moshe made for the Tabernacle, their anointment with the Oil of Anointment sanctified them. From then on, when new utensils were made to replace old ones, *avodatan mechanchatan* — their *first* use in the Temple service inaugurated them as holy vessels of the *Beit Hamikdash*."

While it is true that normally it would be permissible to kindle the *Menorah* with the defiled oil; this applies only when there is a holy *Menorah* which needs to be kindled. However, when the Hasmoneans regained control over the *Beit Hamikdash*, at that time there wasn't a *mitzvah* of kindling the *Menorah* since they did not have the *Menorah* and had to make a new one. Thus, the newly constructed *Menorah* was to be considered as inaugurated for Temple use with the kindling. This can only be accomplished with oil without any trace of defilement.

(כלי חמדה פ׳ בהעלותך, עי׳ קונטרס נס השמן ענף א׳)

* * *

A proof to the theory that in a time of *chinuch* — dedication — a more sublime standard is required can be derived from the first dedication of the *Kohanim* which took place in the wilderness in the days of Moshe.

On the day when Aharon and his four sons were being inaugurated as *Kohanim* in the *Mishkan* — Tabernacle — tragedy befell Nadav and Avihu and they suddenly expired. The Torah (*Vayikra* 10:4-5) relates that "Moshe summoned Mishael and Eltzafan (who were Levites), sons of Aharon's uncle Uziel, and said to them, 'Approach, carry out your brothers (relatives) out of the Sanctuary to the outside of the camp.'" Moshe also instructed Elazar and Itamar (who were *Kohanim*), "Do not leave your heads unshorn and do not rend your garments."

Commentaries ask, while it is true that a *Kohen Gadol* is forbidden to defile himself for even his closest relatives and he must not practice mourning, an ordinary *Kohen* may attend the funeral of a brother and practice the laws of mourning. If so, why did Moshe call in the Levite cousins and not instruct Elazar and Itamar, who were only ordinary *Kohanim*, to carry out their expired brothers? Also, why did he tell Elazar and Itamar not to leave their hair unshorn and not to rend their garments?

The *Da'at Zekeinim Miba'alei Hatosafot* answers that even a *Kohen Hedyot* — ordinary *Kohen* — has the laws of a *Kohen Gadol* on the day he is anointed and inaugurated as a *Kohen*. Since this was the day of their inauguration, they were forbidden to defile themselves even for a brother.

From this we see that at the time of *chinuch* — inauguration into service — things are on a much loftier level than usual and a higher standard of purity is required. Thus, the Hasmoneans did not settle for "permitted *tumah*" since it is not the supreme *taharah* — purity — needed on the day of the inauguration of the new *Menorah*.

(גליוני הש״ס מר׳ יוסף ז״ל ענגעל, חכמת שלמה על גליון השו״ע סי׳ עת״ר)

"טמאו כל השמנים שבהיכל"
"They defiled all the oils that were in the Sanctuary."

QUESTION: In the *Gemara* (*Pesachim* 17a) there is an opinion that *mashkei Beit Midbechaya* — liquids of the Altar — (wine and oil belonging to the *Beit Hamikdash*) are not susceptible to *tumah* — defilement — and of course cannot cause defilement to other things. If so, how did the oil of the *Menorah* become defiled?

ANSWER: The *Gemara* (*Avodah Zarah* 52b) says that the Greeks defiled the Altar by using it to sacrifice offerings to an idol. Since it is written "And lawless people came into it [the Sanctuary] and profaned it" (Ezekiel 7:22), once the gentile idolaters entered the Sanctuary, all the Temple's utensils were stripped of their sanctify.

The law that liquids of the *Beit Hamikdash* are not susceptible to defilement is applicable only as long as the Holiness of the *Beit Hamikdash* is intact, but not when it has lost its sanctity due to gentile idolaters.

(שו״ת בית יצחק סי׳ ק״ו ועי׳ בקונטרס נס השמן)

WHICH *KOHEN GADOL* SEALED IT?

"פך אחד של שמן שהיה מונח בחותמו של כהן גדול"
"One flask of oil that lay there with the *Kohen Gadol's* seal."

QUESTION: What exactly was the flask of oil, and which *Kohen Gadol's* seal did it bear?

ANSWER: The Torah relates that when Yaakov set out to meet his brother Eisav, he had his family cross over the stream, and he sent over all his possessions. [Then], *"vayivateir Yaakov levado"* — "Yaakov remained alone" (*Bereishit* 32:25). Rashi cites a *Gemara* (*Chullin* 91a) that actually Yaakov crossed over the stream together with his family but had forgotten some *"pachim ketanim"* — small earthenware jugs —

and he returned to fetch them. Thus, the word *"levado"* — "alone" — is read as *"lekado"* — "for his jug" (see *Da'at Zekeinim Miba'alei Hatosafot*).

The reason that Yaakov endangered himself for these seemingly inexpensive possessions was that when he was traveling from Beer-Sheva to Charan he slept over on Mount Moriah, where eventually the *Beit Hamikdash* would be built. Early in the morning he took the stone that he placed around his head and set it up as a pillar, and he poured oil on its top (Ibid. 28:18). This oil was from a jug which miraculously appeared to him. After pouring from it on the stone, it miraculously filled itself up again. Years later this jug of oil was used to anoint the Tabernacle and its vessels, Aaron the *Kohen Gadol* and his sons, and also kings. The container of oil is still existing in its entirety, and it will be used to anoint King *Mashiach* (see *Shemot* 30:31, Rashi, Ramban). Yaakov thus realized that it was special oil which was destined for blessings, and he decided not to leave it there. When he realized that he had forgotten the oil, he risked his life to go back and retrieve it.

(שפתי כהן עה"ת פ׳ וישלח)

This jug was the single flask of oil that miraculously appeared to the Hasmoneans and though it was sufficient only for one night's kindling, it lasted for eight nights. The flask bore the seal of Aharon the *Kohen Gadol*.

(ברכת שמואל פ׳ מקץ מר׳ אהרן שמואל ז"ל קיידינובר, פפד"מ תמ"כ, ועי׳ מדבר קדמות להחיד"א)

* * *

According to another opinion it bore the seal of the Patriarch Yaakov, who was also considered a *Kohen Gadol*.

(אור התורה לר׳ יחיאל מאיר זצ"ל מ׳אסטראווצא, ע"י ילקוט שמעוני בראשית קל"ב, עה"פ ויגע בכף ירכו, א"ל הקב"ה למיכאל יפה עשית שעשית כהן שלי בעל מום" ועי׳ במד"ר בראשית פ"ע ה׳ שיעקב בקש לחם הפנים ובגדי כהונה, ועי׳ מד"ר פמ"ו, ה׳, אברהם כהן גדול היה שנאמר (תהלים ק"י:ד) נשבע ה׳ ולא ינחם אתה כהן לעולם וגו׳)

* * *

Of course, the popular opinion is that the flask of oil had on it the seal of Matityahu.

(עי׳ בני יששכר מאמר ד׳ אות ט"ו)

This can also serve as another answer to the *Beit Yosef's* question that the Festival of *Chanukah* should be only seven days since they had a flask of oil that was sufficient for one day. In reality the Syrian-Greeks defiled *all* the oils, and there was not even a single flask of pure oil. However, miraculously this flask appeared, and it lasted for eight days until a new supply arrived.

(ים התלמוד עמ״ס בבא קמא, בהקדמה)

* * *

Incidentally, according to a *midrash*, Hashem said to Yaakov, "You endangered yourself to return for a small jug for my sake (the jug of oil he used to pour on the pillar); I will personally repay your descendants in the time of the Hasmoneans when a miracle will be performed with a small jug."

This shows another connection between Yaakov and *Chanukah*. See page 126.

(צידה לדרך בשם המהרש״ל)

BEIT YOSEF'S QUESTION: WHY CELEBRATE EIGHT DAYS?

"ולא היה בו אלא להדליק יום אחד,
נעשה בו נס והדליקו ממנו שמונה ימים "

"The oil in the flask was sufficient for only one day, but miraculously they kindled from it for eight days."

QUESTION: Since the flask of oil found was sufficient for the first day, the miracle was for only seven days, so why is *Chanukah* celebrated eight days?

ANSWER: The *Beit Yosef* (*Tur, Orach Chaim* 670) provides three answers for this problem:

1) The Hasmoneans knew that it would take them eight days to get a new supply of oil. They did not want to kindle the *Menorah* for merely one night and neglect the succeeding seven nights. Hence, they decided to divide the flask of oil

into eight equal parts. Miraculously, the small amount of oil used the first night lasted for the entire night, and this happened again each of the succeeding seven nights.

2) After filling the *Menorah* on the first night, they saw that the flask remained full of oil. This miracle reoccurred for the next seven nights.

3) In the evening they poured the entire flask of oil into the *Menorah* and kindled it. In the morning, they were amazed to find that after burning the entire night the cups were still filled with oil. Thus, on the first night a miracle had already occurred.

* * *

Some difficulties with the above:

1) Only pure olive oil is suitable, and not oil derived through a miracle!

2) The *Menorah* cups must be filled with enough oil to last the night (*Menachot* 89a).

Enhanced Quality

In response, Rabbi Chaim Soloveichik of Brisk advances the thought that on the first night the *entire* flask of oil was poured into the *Menorah*. The miracle was in the *quality* of the oil. Oil which normally could burn for one night suddenly acquired the power to last for eight nights. Thus, each night the *Menorah* remained full, with the original olive oil losing only 1/8th of its "flame" potentiality.

(במועדים בהלכה מייחס הנ״ל להגר״ח ז״ל מבריסק, וברשימות כ״ק אדמו״ר חוברת ג׳ מייחסו להצ״צ)

Miracle Oil is Kosher

The Lubavitcher Rebbe questioned the need for the explanation that the oil did not increase in quantity but rather was enhanced in quality, since otherwise there is a difficulty that only pure olive oil is suitable and not oil derived through a miracle.

He opines that when the Torah prescribed *shemen zayit* —
it was not to exclude miracle oil. It was merely because the
Torah wanted the best quality among oils, and olive oil
produces the most clean and constant flame. If oil of such
nature was produced through a miracle, there is absolutely
nothing wrong with using it for the *Menorah* kindling.

There is a question in *Gemara* (*Menachot* 69b) concerning
wheat which miraculously came down from the clouds: Can it
be used for the two loaves offered on *Shavuot?* The *Gemara*
concludes that it cannot, which would seem to suggest that
only items of natural origin are suitable in the *Beit Hamikdash*
and not something produced by a miracle?

This does not contradict the above conclusion since there
the question is that the Torah wrote an extra word
"mimoshvoteichem" — "from your settled places" (*Vayikra*
23:17). We thus ponder whether it means to exclude
specifically wheat from *chutz la'eretz* — Diaspora — but not if
it is from the clouds, or is it a prerequisite that the wheat
must have grown in *Eretz Yisrael* and any other wheat (even if
it came down from clouds and is of equal quality) is
excluded. However, when the Torah wrote *"shemen zayit"* —
"olive oil" — the word *"zayit"* — "olive" — is not superfluous
because it is necessary to exclude other inferior oils but it
does not exclude miraculous oil which has the identical
qualities of natural olive oil.

(רשימות כ״ק אדמו״ר ח״ג)

* * *

This answers the first question (regarding miracle oil)
raised on the *Beit Yosef's* explanation.

As for the second question [that the *Menorah* must be
filled with enough oil for the night] this is only *lechat'chilah* —
a priori — based on the reason that *"Ein aniyut bimkom
ashirut"* — "There should be no manifestation of poverty in a
place of opulence." However, possessing only one flask of
suitable oil exemplifies extreme poverty. Therefore, dividing

it and relying on a miracle to occur is proper in such a situation.

(עי' ספר נר למאה סי' ט"ו, ובקונטרס נס השמן ענף ה')

ANOTHER DIFFICULTY WITH *BEIT YOSEF'S* EXPLANATION

QUESTION: According to the *Beit Yosef's* explanation that immediately after filling the cups of the *Menorah* the flask filled up again, this repeated itself up to the seventh day. Thus, *Chanukah* should only be for seven days since no miracle occurred on the eighth day?

ANSWER: The miracle was not that they emptied the entire flask into the seven cups of the *Menorah* and then the empty flask miraculously filled up again. Rather, as they were pouring the oil into the *Menorah,* what was poured out was immediately miraculously replaced. Thus, already on the first day after the first bit was poured out of the flask, the flask held a mixture of original oil and miraculous oil. Consequently, for all the eight nights of *Chanukah* the *Menorah* was kindled with the mixture, and even on the first night it was impossible to ascertain if the oil used was totally the original which was found or some of the oil that came into the flask by way of miracle. Hence, the kindling of *all* eight days was partially with miracle oil and therefore we celebrate for eight days.

(חכמת שלמה על גליון השו"ע סי' עת"ר)

Alternatively, even if we should say that the flask refilled itself after it was emptied into the *Menorah,* the reason to celebrate eight days is that this occurred also on the eighth night after they filled the *Menorah* cups. Thus, they witnessed a miracle also on the eighth day although they did not use this oil on the ninth day since a fresh supply had already arrived.

(נרות שמונה)

FOUR ADDITIONAL ANSWERS TO *BEIT YOSEF's* QUESTION

1) 25th Commemorates Victory

The *Pri Chadash* explains that if it were only for the miracle of the oil, then *Chanukah* would only be seven days. The eight-day celebration has two reasons: The 25th of *Kislev* is celebrated because of the miraculous victory the Hasmoneans experienced in the war, and the other seven days mark the seven days of miraculous *Menorah* kindling.

(פרי חדש סי׳ עת״ר)

2) 25th Commemorates Finding Oil

In reality there was no miracle in the first day and the eight days of celebration is not *only* because of the kindling of the *Menorah* until new oil was provided.

The first day (25 *Kislev*) was declared a *Yom Tov* in order to thank Hashem for delivering us from the Syrian-Greek oppressors and for helping us find the one flask of undefiled oil. The additional seven days of *Chanukah* commemorate the miracle that oil sufficient for only one day miraculously lasted an additional seven days when there was no other oil available.

(מאירי)

QUESTION: A difficulty raised with these two explanations is as follows: Why is the *Menorah* kindled eight days — the kindling should have started on the 26th of *Kislev* for a period of seven days?

ANSWER: The Hasmoneans fought strictly for spiritual reasons. The Syrian-Greeks endeavored to cause the Jews to stop learning Torah and cease doing *mitzvot*. Unfortunately, they were somewhat successful and many Jews became Hellenized. Cognizant that the Jews were facing spiritual devastation, the Hasmoneans went to war and the victory was not for physical or material matters but strictly a spiritual victory for Torah and *mitzvoth*.

Hence, when the Rabbis declared the 25th of *Kislev* as a *Yom Tov* for the victory, they ordained that it be celebrated with candles and light since candles corresponds to *mitzvot* and light corresponds to Torah, as King Shlomo said, "For a *mitzvah* is a candle and Torah is light" (Proverbs 6:23).

(רשימות כ״ק אדמו״ר ח״ג ע' 18)

3) 25th Commemorates "Fire from Heaven"

The *Gemara* says that though the *Kohanim* would light a fire on the Altar, a fire also descended from heaven which consumed the sacrifices. This fire was also there during the second *Beit Hamikdash,* although it did not assist in consuming the sacrifices placed on the Altar (*Yoma* 21b). When the Syrian-Greeks entered the Sanctuary, they defiled the Altar by sacrificing an idol on it, and thus the heavenly fire departed.

Upon gaining entry to the Sanctuary, on the 25th of *Kislev,* the *Kohanim* dedicated a new Altar, but to their great disappointment no heavenly fire descended upon it.

After much praying, a heavenly fire appeared between the stones of the Altar (see Josephus, ch. 20). Prior to the evening of the 26th of *Kislev* they kindled the *Menorah* for the first time (see Rambam, *Chanukah* 3:2) and the flask of oil lasted them for eight days, until new pure oil was received.

Thus, the eight-day celebration which commences on the 25th of *Kislev* commemorates two events: the first day commemorates Hashem's response to their prayers and sending a fire from heaven, and the seven succeeding days commemorate seven days of miraculous *Menorah* kindling.

(מחזיק ברכה לההחיד״א סי' עת״ר:א)

A difficulty can be raised; if the celebration on the first day is for the heavenly fire that descended on the Altar, why do we light the *Menorah* on the night of the 25th?

The answer may be because the *Gemara* (*Yoma* 45b) says that from the *Aish Tamid* — constant fire — that was on the Altar they would take fire for the kindling of the *Menorah*.

Thus, when the *Kohanim* dedicated the Altar and there was no heavenly fire they were greatly disappointed. Afterwards, when the heavenly fire appeared, they rejoiced, since they would be able to use it for the kindling of the *Menorah*. Hence, we kindle the *Menorah* to celebrate the miracle of heavenly fire appearing on the Altar which was used later in the day to kindle the *Menorah*.

(ויחי יוסף - ר' יוסף זצ"ל מפאפא)

4) Flask Was *Not* Enough for 25th

According to the *Mechilta D'rav Achai, Vayishlach*, the flask of oil found was *not* enough for even one night's kindling. Thus, already on the 25th they experienced a miracle when the *Menorah* burned the entire night. Therefore, *Chanukah* is celebrated with *Menorah* kindling for eight days, to commemorate the eight day of miraculous *Menorah* kindling.

A difficulty with the *Mechilta* is the following: The *Menorah* had to be lit for the entire night — why would the flasks of oil prepared for the daily kindling contain less than what is needed for the required lighting time?

In describing the miracle of *Chanukah*, the *Gemara* relates that the Jews found only one flask of oil and that it had the seal of the *Kohen Gadol*. In the *Beit Hamikdash* there were *Kohanim* assigned to the special task of making oil, and it was not the responsibility of the *Kohen Gadol* to make oil. Why then did this particular flask bear the *Kohen Gadol's* seal?

The *Kohen Gadol* was required to bring a daily meal-offering consisting of flour and oil, known as "*chavitei Kohen Gadol*" (*Vayikra* 6:15). Normally, the oil used for this offering would be of lower quality than that used for the kindling of the *Menorah* (*Shemot* 27:20, Rashi). However, the *Kohen Gadol* in that time was a highly distinguished spiritual personality, and a *mehader bemitzvot* — one scrupulous in *mitzvot* — who used *pure* olive oil for his daily sacrifice.

When the Hasmoneans entered the *Beit Hamikdash*, they did not find any pure olive oil to kindle the *Menorah*. Luckily, they found one flask which was designated for the *Kohen*

Gadol's daily sacrifice, and, to their utter amazement, it was pure olive oil.

The *Menorah* required one half *lug* (5 ½ oz.) for each of the seven candles, adding up to a total of 3 ½ *lugim* (*Menachot* 88a). The *Kohen Gadol's* daily sacrifice required only a total of three *lugim* of oil per day (*Menachot* 87b). Thus, the flask found was *not* sufficient for even one night, though miraculously it burnt through the entire night.

(שפת אמת – מלא העומר מר' ארי' ליב ז"ל צינץ)

Alternatively, the *Gemara* (*Avodah Zarah* 43a) says that the Syrian-Greeks plundered the vessels of the *Beit Hamikdash,* including the *Menorah.* After the Jews chased them out, they make a *Menorah* of wood. New wood has a tendency to absorb oil until it becomes saturated. Thus, actually when the flask of oil was prepared the content was enough for one night, assuming that it was poured into the regular *Menorah* whose cups were fully saturated and no longer absorbing oil. However, now that they had to kindle the new wooden *Menorah,* the content of the flask was not enough even for one night's kindling, and nevertheless it miraculously burnt throughout the entire night.

(חידושי מהרצ"א)

FIVE ADDITIONAL ANSWERS TO *BEIT YOSEF'S* QUESTIONS

On 25th Some Oil Remained in Flask

1) The *Taz* explains that according to the *Zohar,* in order for a miracle to occur, there must first be something tangible in existence. Thus, after filling the *Menorah* with oil from the flask, which had a sufficient amount for just one day, some oil remained in the flask. Miraculously, this little bit of oil which remained in the flask increased till the flask was full and sufficient for the kindling of the next evening. This miracle repeated itself every evening after filling the *Menorah.* Hence, immediately on the first day a miracle occurred.

(טורי זהב סי' עת"ר)

* * *

Without the One there Wouldn't be Seven

2) The reason for 8 days though they had oil for the first day can be explained with a parable: A businessman once traveled to a market with eight bags of gold coins. While he was staying over at an inn, bandits stole seven of them. Immediately he took money from the one remaining bag and hired people to catch the bandits and vowed to Hashem that if the search was successful he would donate ten percent of the money to charity. They skillfully made an investigation and apprehended the thieves.

When the *gabba'ei tzedakah* — people in charge of *tzedakah* funds — arrived to collect their due, a debate arose concerning whether he had to give charity from all eight bags of gold coins or only from seven? It was decided that he should give from all eight, for were it not for the eighth bag that miraculously remained in his possession, he would have been penniless and without funds to hire people to pursue the bandits and recover his money.

The same is true with celebrating eight days. Though the Jews had a flask with sufficient oil for one night, were it not for that one flask that was found, there would have not been any oil to miraculously burn for eight days.

(פון אונזער אלטען אוצר בשם קומץ המנחה)

8 Days to Distinguish Between *Beit Hillel* and *Beit Shammai*

3) There is an argument in the *Gemara* (*Shabbat* 21b) as to how many candles should be lit each night of *Chanukah*. According to *Beit Hillel*, we start the first night with one candle and each night we add a candle. According to *Beit Shammai*, we start the first night with eight, and decrease by one every night after.

According to the *Avudraham*, one of the meanings of the name "*Chanukah*" is "חי נרות והלכה כבית הללי" — "Candles should be lit for eight days, and the *halachah* is according to *Beit Hillel*" (that each night we increase one candle).

When one looks at the *Chanukah Menorah* any day of
Chanukah, one can immediately tell from the number of
candles being lit, that the *halachah* is according to *Beit Hillel.*

For example, on the third day of *Chanukah* one sees three
candles lit, and one knows that this is according to *Beit Hillel,*
because according to *Beit Shammai,* there should have been six
candles lit. On the sixth day of *Chanukah,* if one sees six
candles lit, one can derive from this that the *halachah* is
according to *Beit Hillel,* because according to *Beit Shammai*
there should have been only three candles lit.

If *Chanukah* candles were only lit for a period of seven
days, then on the fourth night of *Chanukah,* according to *Beit
Hillel* and also according to *Beit Shammai,* a total of only four
candles would be lit. Thus, if one looked at the *Chanukah
Menorah* that evening, one would not be able to see if the
halachah was according to *Beit Hillel* or *Beit Shammai.* However,
when *Chanukah* is celebrated for eight days, then on the
fourth day, according to *Beit Hillel* one lights four candles and
according to *Beit Shammai* one lights five candles.

Since the word *"Chanukah"* indicates that the *halachah* is
according to *Beit Hillel, Chanukah* has to be eight days and not
seven days.

(ברכת חיים)

8 Days for 8 Yomim Tovim

"קבעום ועשאום ימים טובים בהלל והודאה"

**"They established and rendered these
eight days as festival days with respect to
reciting *Hallel* and thanksgiving."**

4) QUESTION: It should say that they established these
eight days as a *Yom Tov* — holiday — in singular; why does it
say *"Yomim Tov"* — "holidays" — in plural?

ANSWER: One of the things the Syrian-Greeks
demanded of the Jews was that they abolish *Rosh Chodesh.*
They sought that their calendar should not be dependant on

the *Beit Din's* sanctifying the new moon each month based on the testimony of witnesses, but rather it should be in accordance with the solar system, as the calendar of the entire world.

The dates the Torah prescribes for the observance of a *Yom Tov* are based on the lunar system. Hence, without a calendar based on the moon we would not know when to observe any *Yom Tov,* and thus, *Yomim Tovim* would be forgotten.

In *Eretz Yisrael* there are eight days during the year which are observed as *Yom Tov. Pesach* is celebrated on the first and seventh days of the festival, the 15th and 21st of *Nissan. (Chol Hamoeid* — the intermediate days — is not considered *Yom Tov;* see *Turei Zahav* 668:1) *Shavuot* is celebrated one day on the 6th of *Sivan. Rosh Hashanah* — even in *Eretz Yisrael* — is always celebrated for two days: the first and second day of *Tishrei* (see *Rosh Hashanah* 30b). *Yom Kippur* is only one day, on the 10th of *Tishrei,* and *Sukkot* and *Shemini Atzeret* are one day each: the 15th and 22nd day of *Tishrei.* Thus, had the Syrian-Greeks, G-d forbid, achieved their desires, the Jewish people would be missing eight days of *Yomim Tovim.*

Thanks to the defeat of the enemy, the Jews were then able to celebrate and observe all the *Yomim Tovim* — holidays — without any fear. Consequently, when the *Sanhedrin* established the celebration of the victory of the Hasmoneans, they made it for eight days of *Yomim Tovim* (plural) corresponding to the eight days of various *Yomim Tovim* the Syrian-Greeks wanted to stop the Jewish people from celebrating. They did not, however, forbid working, but rather emphasized *Hallel* and thanksgiving to Hashem.

(חתן סופר על חנוכה סי׳ י״ט)

8 Days for 8 Divine Salvations

5) In *Shemoneh Esreih* and *Birkat Hamazon* we recite, during *Chanukah,* the prayer of *Al Hanissim.* In it, there are a total of *eight* things mentioned which Hashem did in our behalf to

make *Chanukah* a reality. "You... 1) waged their battles, 2) defended their rights, 3) avenged the wrong done to them, 4) delivered the mighty into the hand of the weak, 5) the many into the hand of the few, 6) the impure into the hand of the pure, 7) the wicked into the hand of the righteous, 8) and wanton sinners into the hand of those who occupy themselves with Your Torah."

Therefore, *Chanukah* is celebrated eight days, though the miracle of the oil was only for seven days.

(ספר נר למאה בשם זכר אברהם)

For more answers to *Beit Yosef's* question, see pages 31, 109, 172, 181, 182.

WHY NOT 9 DAYS

"בכ״ה בכסליו יומי דחנוכה תמניא אינון"

"On the 25th of *Kislev* [begin] the days of *Chanukah,* eight in number."

QUESTION: Because of a doubt as to which days the *Beit Din* declared as *Rosh Chodesh* in the Diaspora every *Yom-Tov* is celebrated two days. Why isn't *Chanukah,* too, nine days in Diaspora?

ANSWER: All *Yomim Tovim* except for *Chanukah* and *Purim,* are Biblical. There is more stringency concerning a doubt related to a Biblical matter than one concerning something Rabbinical. Therefore, out of doubt as to what day is actually the first of the month, the *Yom-Tov* is celebrated for two days. This stringency is not extended, however, to *Yomim Tovim* which are merely of Rabbinical origin.

(אבודרהם)

Some say that really *Chanukah* should only have been seven days since without any miracles there was sufficient oil in the flask they found for one night. Thus, the eighth day was added only because of the doubt of which day in the month was designated as the day of *Rosh Chodesh.* Hence, there is no need for a ninth day because the eighth day was already added to satisfy the doubt.

(ערבי נחל)

A difficulty with this is that we might wonder. If so, why *Chanukah* is also eight days in *Eretz Yisrael?*

(חתם סופר)

Others claim that the reason for two days of *Yom Tov* is that after the *Beit Din* in *Eretz Yisrael* declared *Rosh Chodesh* they would dispatch emissaries to notify the people who lived far away from *Yerushalayim* and in the Diaspora which day was established. Since it would take them more than fifteen days to reach the community, the people would celebrate *Yom-Tov* for two days. However, by the 25th of the month they would definitely reach even the most distant Jewish community and thus there is no need for a ninth day because of any doubts.

(ברכי יוסף סי׳ עת״ר, וצ״ע דתנן בר״ה דף י״ח ע״א ששלוחים יצאו בכסלו מפני חנוכה)

Nevertheless, there is an opinion that indeed in those days *Chanukah* was only eight days in *Eretz Yisrael* (where every *Yom Tov* lasted for one day). However, in the distant communities where every *Yom-Tov* was celebrated two days because the messengers would not arrive in time to inform them which day was declared *Rosh Chodesh, Chanukah* too was celebrated for nine days.

Now that we have a pre-calculated calendar and we observe two days *Yom Tov* only because of *"Minhag avoteinu beyadeinu"* — we follow the customs of our parents (see Rambam, *Kiddush HaChodesh* 5:5) — we are stringent to do as our parents did only in regard to a Biblical *Yom Tov* but not in regard to *Chanukah*, which is only of Rabbinic origin.

However, when the *Beit Hamikdash* will be rebuilt and we will return to the establishment of *Rosh Chodesh* by *Beit Din* based on the testimony of witnesses, then *Chanukah* in Diaspora will again be nine days.

(מנחת חינוך מצוה ש״א, ועי׳ במועדים בהלכה – חנוכה סי׳ ב)

Another explanation for *Chanukah's* not having nine days is that we celebrate for eight days because the Syrian-Greeks decreed against *Shabbat, Rosh Chodesh* and *milah* — circumcision. Therefore, the Rabbis decided that the celebration be for eight-days since in an eight day period there is a *Shabbat*, a *Rosh Chodesh (Tevet)*, and a possibility for *brit milah* on the eighth day for a child born during *Chanukah*. If *Chanukah* were celebrated for nine days, the whole idea expressed by eight days would be obscured.

(חדרי בטן להחיד״א, מקץ אות ט״ו)

25TH OR 26TH?

"בכ״ה בכסליו יומי דחנוכה תמניא אינון"

"On the 25th of *Kislev* the days of *Chanukah* commence, they are eight days in all."

QUESTION: On what day was the war actually won, and when did the first *Menorah* kindling take place?

ANSWER: According to one opinion, the victory was declared on the 24th of *Kislev*. Towards evening of the 25th the *Menorah* was kindled and it burned through the entire night, and in the morning they brought offerings on the Altar. Thus, the name "*Chanukah*" which can be read "*Chanu chof hei*" — "They rested on the 25th" — means that the 25th was the first complete day of rest after a long, tedious battle.

(מאירי)

The Rambam (*Chanukah* 3:2) writes, "When the Jews overpowered their enemies and destroyed them it was on the 25th of *Kislev*, and they entered the Sanctuary and found no non-defiled oil in the Sanctuary except for one flask which was sufficient for only one day, and they kindled with it the candles for eight days until olives were crushed and clean oil was produced."

Accordingly, there was fighting still on the 25th and sometime during the day, victory was declared and they rested on *part* of the 25th day. On the 25th late in the afternoon they kindled the *Menorah* and it burned through the night of the 26th.

Then the Rambam writes in the next *halachah* (3:3) "Therefore, the Sages of that generation declared that these eight days which commence from the night of the 25th of *Kislev* should be days of happiness and joy, and candles are lit in the evening at the entrance doors to the houses every night of the eight nights to demonstrate and publicize the miracle."

The Rambam seems to be contradicting himself! If the *Menorah* was first lit on the 25th, and if it burned throughout the night of the 26th, shouldn't the commemorative annual kindling commence on the eve of the 26th?

Some explain that according to the Rambam, we kindle on the eve of the 25th to commemorate the victory that took place on that day and the remaining seven nights of kindling is to commemorate the seven day miraculous kindling of the *Menorah* after the flask of oil was consumed.

(פרי חדש סי' עת"ר, א)

A difficulty still remains, why is the victory celebrated with kindling the *Menorah?*

An explanation may be the following: According to the Jewish calendar, the day starts with evening, as the Torah says, "And there was evening and there was morning one day" (*Bereishit* 1:5). However, the *Gemara* (*Chullin* 83a) says that in regard to matters of the holiness of the *Beit Hamikdash* it is the reverse. Day starts with morning and the evening is a continuation of the day. This is evident from the verse "[The offering] must be eaten on the day of its offering; he may not leave any of it until morning" (*Vayikra* 7:15). Since it may be eaten the entire night until the morning and since the Torah calls this *"beyom karbano"* — "in the *day* of his offering" — it is evident that in regard to holiness the night is a continuation of the day it follows (Rashi).

Thus, though the *Menorah* lighting took place on the eve of the 26th, since this was a matter of the holiness of the *Beit Hamikdash,* it is associated with the 25th day. However, our kindling at the entrance to our houses is not a matter of "holiness." Therefore since our day commences with the evening, it cannot be considered as associated with the 25th day unless it be done on the eve of the 25th.

(לקו״ש ח״ל ע׳ 204)

Alternatively, according to the *Rambam* (*Temidim Umusafim* 3:12) the *Menorah* was lit twice a day, in the late afternoon, and again in the morning. Thus, victory was declared early in the morning of the 25th of *Kislev,* and immediately the *Kohanim* went to the *Beit Hamikdash* and they did the morning lighting of the *Menorah.*

Now according to the Rambam the victory was as follows; on the 25th of *Kislev* they found the single flask of oil which was sufficient only for one kindling and they used it for the morning kindling. Miraculously, this flask provided oil for *both* the evening and morning kindling of the next seven days. Hence, on each of the eight days of *Chanukah* a miracle was experienced.

A question, however, can be raised; the *Gemara* (*Avodah Zarah* 43a) says that they made a new wooden *Menorah.* Hence, it needed to be sanctified, and the *Gemara* (*Menachot* 49a) says that the sanctifying of the *Menorah* can only be done with the evening lighting. If so how were they able to kindle on the morning of the 25th?

The *halachah* that sanctification can only be accomplished with evening kindling is a Rabbinic ordination.

It could be that the need for a new *Menorah* was not because the old one was plundered but rather because it was defiled since it was used for idol worship, the same as the Altar which was stored away and replaced with a new one for that reason (see *Avodah Zarah* 52b). Since the prohibition to use such vessels is only a Rabbinical law, and kindling *Menorah* is a

Biblical command, the Rabbis made their ruling only when an alternative exists.

Consequently, for the morning kindling they had no other alternative but to use the old *Menorah.* For the evening lighting, however, they used the new wooden *Menorah,* which they were able to sanctify with its inauguration into service for the evening kindling, as the *Gemara* (*Shevuout* 15a) says, "*Avodatan mechanchatan*" — The vessels become sanctified through their first use for service in the *Beit Hamikdash.*

(אור גדול על משניות יומא פ״ז מ״ד)

SIGNIFICANCE OF 36 CANDLES

"נעשה בו נס והדליקו ממנו שמונה ימים"

"A miracle occurred with it, and they kindled with it for eight days."

QUESTION: To commemorate this miracle we kindle a total of 36 candles during *Chanukah* (excluding the *Shamashim*). What is the significance of the 36 candles of *Chanukah?*

ANSWER: The *Gemara* (*Chagigah* 12a) says regarding the light that Hashem created on the first day that man could use it to survey everything from one end of the world to the other. Once, however, He looked at the Generation of the Flood and the Generation of the Dispersion and He saw that their deeds were perverse, He proceeded to hide the light from them, and hid it for the righteous people in the future. According to the *Zohar* (*Shemot* 148-49) not only will the righteous enjoy it in the World to Come in the Messianic Era, but it is hidden in the Torah. Whenever people exert themselves in the study of Torah, a ray shines forth from that light and rests upon them.

When the miracle of *Chanukah* occurred and the *Menorah* was kindled with the oil of the flask, Hashem revealed some of the exalted hidden light of the future. Also, on every

Chanukah, during the kindling of the *Menorah*, there is a revealing of the hidden light — the light of *Mashiach*.

The name *"Chanukah"* etymologically stems from the word *"chinuch"* — education and preparation. A parent educates and prepares a young child prior to the time when he will be obligated to perform *mitzvot* so he will have all the knowledge he needs when the time actually comes. Likewise, Hashem reveals on *Chanukah* some of the "hidden light" which we will enjoy in the exalted days of *Mashiach*.

According to the *Midrash* (*Rabbah Bereishit* 11:2) the great light which Hashem created functioned for Adam a total of 36 hours: twelve hours on Friday day and the twenty four hours of *Shabbat*. In addition, the words *"ohr"* — "light" — or *"neir"* — "candle" — or *"me'orot"* — "luminaries" — appear in the Torah a total of 36 times. The Greeks wanted to stop us from studying Torah and thus fail to benefit from the great light which is hidden in the Torah, and which served Adam for 36 hours. Therefore, on *Chanukah*, when Hashem reveals to us some of the great light that will radiate in the days of *Mashiach*, the custom is to light a total of 36 candles (without the *shamashim*).

(בני יששכר בשם הרוקח)

Alternatively, the Syrian-Greeks endeavored to cause the Jews *"lehashkicham Toratecha"* — to forget the Torah. In the Torah there are two parts, the Written and the Oral. The Written consists of the five volumes of the Torah scroll and the Oral Torah is the *Gemara*, without which we do not really know how to observe the Torah. For example, the Torah says that a Jew should wear *tefillin*. However, without the explanations transmitted from Sinai in the Oral Torah we would not know what *tefillin* are and how to perform the *mitzvah*.

By attempting to stop the Jews from studying the *Gemara* and making them study Greek philosophy and secular studies instead, the Greeks hoped that ultimately the Jews would not know what the Written Torah means, and thus, Torah would be obsolete and forgotten.

In the Babylonian Talmud, there are 36 *Gemarot*. (Some Tractates consist of only *Mishnah* without any *Gemara*, e.g. *Ediyot*). When the Jews conquered their adversaries, they were then able to engage freely in study of the 36 volumes of *Gemara* and thereby assure the continuity of Torah study and observance. In commemoration 36 candles are kindled.

(בני יששכר, ועי' סדר הדורות שמות הספרים אות ת')

"ונעשה בו נס והדליקו ממנו שמונה ימים"

"A miracle occurred with it, and they kindled with it eight days."

QUESTION: Why, in addition to helping the minority of Jews overcome the large number of enemies, did Hashem make the additional miracle connected with candles?

ANSWER: According to the *midrash* (*Rabbah Bereishit* 2:4) the Syrian-Greeks decreed that the Jews cease observing *Shabbat*, circumcision and the sanctification of the new moon to establish the day of *Rosh Chodesh*.

These three *mitzvot* all have an association with candle lighting. *Shabbat* is ushered in with the woman lighting candles and *motza'ei Shabbat* we light the *Havdalah* candle. (In addition, it is customary to light candles on *motza'ei Shabbat* to "escort" the departing *Shabbat* — see *Shulchan Aruch Harav* 300:2, *Ba'eir Heitev* 298:16). At a circumcision it is also customary to kindle candles (see *Sanhedrin* 32b, *Tosafot*).

Based on the acceptance of testimony from witnesses who saw the new moon appear in the sky, the *Beit Din* would decide which day should be designated as *Rosh Chodesh*. To notify the people of the Diaspora, (Babylon) which day was declared *Rosh Chodesh*, so that they would know which day of the month should be celebrated as Yom Tov, torches would be lit on mountaintops on the evening following the day declared as *Rosh Chodesh* (see *Rosh Hashanah* 21b).

Despite the decree of the Syrian-Greeks, the dedicated Jews were unyielding and with *mesirat nefesh* — self sacrifice — continued observing these three *mitzvot*. To demonstrate His love for his devoted people, Hashem specifically made a miracle for them connected with candle lighting.

(משמרת אליעזר)

WHY WASN'T *YOM TOV* DECLARED IMMEDIATELY?

"לשנה אחרת קבעום ועשאום ימים טובים בהלל והודאה"

"In the following year they established and rendered [these eight days] as festival days, with respect to recital of *Hallel* and thanksgiving."

QUESTION: Why was *Purim* immediately declared a *Yom Tov* while *Chanukah* was only declared a holiday the following year?

ANSWER: Haman sought the physical annihilation of the entire Jewish nation. He made his plans during the month of *Nissan* and designated a date a year later, the 13th of *Adar*, as the appropriate time to carry out his insidious plot. During the entire year the Jews prayed and repented, but no one was physically hurt. On the 13th of *Adar*, "the fear of the Jews had fallen upon all the peoples" and "no one stood in their way" when they "struck at all their enemies with the sword, slaughtering and annihilating" (Esther 9:2,5).

On the other hand, the Jews fought the Syrian-Greek armies for three years until they vanquished them and regained control of the *Beit Hamikdash*. During this period there was fierce fighting and many soldiers of the Jewish army were killed. Thus, when the Jews rested on the 25th of *Kislev*, many families were mourning loved ones who had perished. Consequently, it was not deemed proper to immediately declare *Chanukah* as a *Yom Tov*, and the Jews waited till next year, by which time all would have concluded their mourning periods.

(פון אונזער אלטען אוצר בשם פתחי תורה)

Alternatively, when the Rambam (*Chanukah* 3:1) records the events that led up to *Chanukah,* he describes how the Jews suffered bitterly from the Syrian-Greek decrees and their reprehensible conduct in the Sanctuary. He also writes "until the G-d of our fathers had mercy over them and He helped them and saved them, and the children of Chashmonai the *Kohanim Gedolim* overpowered, and they killed them and rescued the Jews from their hands. And they appointed a king from among the *Kohanim,* and the Jewish Kingdom returned to Israel for over two hundred years, until the second destruction [of the *Beit Hamikdash*]." Then the Rambam records the miracle concerning the *Menorah* and concludes (ibid 3:3) "Therefore the Sages of the generation instituted these eight days, which start on the night of the 25th of *Kislev,* as days of *simchah* and *Hallel.*"

Now the Rambam's work is a code of *halachah,* not a history book. What is the relevance to *halachah* that they appointed a king?

The *Gemara* (*Megillah* 14a) says that the reason the Rabbis did not institute the saying of *Hallel* on *Purim* is that the salvation was an incomplete redemption since *"Akati avdei Achashverosh anan"* — "We are still servants of Achashverosh." Though they were relieved of Haman and his cohorts, there was no Jewish government; rather they lived in peace under the rulership of Achashverosh. Regarding *Chanukah,* however, not only were the Jews relieved of the wicked Syrian-Greek oppressors; but after the victory they reinstituted the Jewish kingdom. Hence, at the conclusion of the first anniversary, when they saw that their kingdom was firmly established and thus their victory was a complete redemption, the Rabbis decided to ordain these eight days as a *Yom-Tov* in which *Hallel* is recited.

(תפארת צבי – הרב צבי שי' רוזנטל)

WHY NOT A FEAST?

"ועשאום ימים טובים בהלל והודאה"

"[The eight days] were rendered festival days with respect to recital of *Hallel* and thanksgiving."

QUESTION: Why wasn't *Chanukah* also declared a day of feasting just as *Purim* was?

ANSWER: Haman plotted to annihilate the Jewish people physically. A Jew's religious convictions didn't matter to him. If one was a member of the Jewish people, regardless of age or gender, he wanted that person wiped off the face of the earth. *Chanukah* on the other hand was a totally spiritual war. The ambition of the Syrian-Greeks was "to make them forget Your Torah and violate the decrees of Your will." The Jews who Hellenized and joined with them were to be spared.

Since *Purim* commemorates the salvation of the Jewish people from physical annihilation, the celebration is in a physical form — eating and drinking — things that the body enjoys. In contrast, with regard to *Chanukah,* the Jewish body was not in danger, but rather the soul. Thus, the commemoration and celebration is not expressed by the physical acts of eating and drinking, but by spiritual activities — kindling the *Menorah,* recital of *Hallel,* and thanksgiving.

(ב"ח וט"ז סי' עת"ר)

Alternatively, the feast on *Purim* was instituted for a special reason: Queen Vashti's downfall occurred at the great feast when the King was merry with wine (Esther, 1:10). Queen Esther's coronation was also celebrated with a *mishtei yayin* — feast of wine (2:18). The downfall of Haman and his subsequent execution came about through the wine banquet made by Esther (7:1-10). Therefore, it is a *mitzvah* on *Purim* to have a festive meal at which wine is also consumed.

(אבודרהם, ובמגילה ז' ע"ב רש"י ד"ה לבסומי, כ' "להשתכר ביין")

Alternatively, the *Gemara* (*Shabbat* 88a) says that when Hashem originally gave the Jewish people the Torah, he lifted the mountain over them and forced them to accept it. Nevertheless, they accepted it again willfully in the days of Achashverosh, as it is written 'The Jews established and accepted' (Esther 9:26). They established in the days of Achashverosh that which they had already accepted in the days of Moshe'." [Out of their love for Hashem engendered by the miracle of *Purim* the Jews reaccepted the Torah — Rashi.]

Torah is compared to food and drink, as King Shlomo says, "Come and partake of my bread, and drink the wine that I have mixed" (Proverbs 9:5). Consequently, on *Purim,* which marks our reacceptance of the Torah, we celebrate with festive meals and drinking.

(חי"א)

רעיונות על הלכות חנוכה
Insights on Laws of *Chanukah*

"אמר רב יהודה אמר רב אסי אסור להרצות מעות כנגד נר חנוכה"

"Rav Yehudah said in the name of Rav Assi, 'It is forbidden to count money opposite a *Chanukah* light.'" (*Shabbat* 22a)

QUESTION: The *Gemara* (21b) had already ruled that "it is forbidden to make use of a *Chanukah* candle's light," so what insight did Rav Assi add by specifying not to count money?

ANSWER: The Rambam (*Chanukah* 3:1) describes the events that led up to the miracle of *Chanukah* as follows: "During the time of the second *Beit Hamikdash,* when the Greeks reigned, they issued decrees against the Jews and nullified their laws and did not let them engage in Torah and *mitzvot.* They appropriated their money and daughters, and they entered the Holiness, causing damage and defilement. It was a difficult time for the Jews, and they were under much pressure until Hashem had mercy over them and saved them."

Thus, there was a double salvation: 1) spiritual salvation — they were able to freely study Torah and observe *mitzvot,* and 2) physical salvation — there was no longer any danger or threat to their property. Nevertheless, the Sages declared *Chanukah* as a *Yom Tov* to be celebrated by praising Hashem and thanksgiving and not with festive meals to indicate that the spiritual salvation was primary.

With the *halachah* that it is forbidden to count money opposite a *Chanukah* light, Rav Assi is emphasizing that the celebration is not for the "money" — financial benefits derived through the miracle — but primarily for the spiritual benefit — that the Greeks were no longer able to restrict the Jews in matters of Torah and *mitzvot.*

(שארית מנחם)

"מצותה עד שתכלה רגל מן השוק אמר רבה בר בר חנה
אמר ר' יוחנן עד דכליא ריגלא דתרמודאי"

**"The commandment of *Chanukah* lights
extends until the passersby have vanished from
the market. Rabbah bar bar Chanah said in the
name of Rabbi Yochanan: until the Tarmodians
have vanished from the market." (*Shabbat* 21a)**

QUESTION: The Tarmodians were a group of people who
sold kindling wood in the city markets. They remained
longest in the market until the people returned home in the
evening to start their fires and those in need of kindling wood
returned to the market to purchase it.

Since the *Gemara* already said that the kindling continues
until the passersby vanish from the market, what insight did
Rabbah bar bar Chanah give us by identifying the passersby?

ANSWER: Perhaps the statement of Rabbah bar bar
Chanah can be explained as a metaphor.

The purpose of lighting *Chanukah* candles is to illuminate
the dark and gloomy "outside" world. The Syrian-Greeks
endeavored to "darken" the Jewish scene by prohibiting the
Jews to study Torah and perform *mitzvot*. To counteract this,
our Sages instructed us to go "out" into the darkness of the
street and illuminate it with the *Chanukah* candles. Candles
are an allusion to Torah and *mitzvot*, as the *pasuk* says "for a
candle is a *mitzvah* and Torah is light" (Proverbs 6:23).
Through bringing the light of Torah and *mitzvot* to the
alienated, and prevailing on them to conduct their lives in
accordance with Torah teaching, the "darkness" of the world
is dispelled and it becomes a spiritually illuminated area.

The Kabbalists note that the word *"Tarmod"* (תרמוד) can be
rearranged to read (מורדת) *"moredet"* — "rebel." In fact, the
Tarmodians were once slaves of King Shlomo who rebelled
(see *Yevamot* 17a).

Rabbah bar bar Chanah is telling us that one must
continue to light *Chanukah* candles until he has illuminated
the outside to the extent that *rigla detarmuda'ei* — the feet of

the rebels who are circulating among the public and influencing them to rebel against Hashem and cease observing Torah and *mitzvot* — are nullified and eradicated. Moreover, the rebels who wanted to arrange a mutiny and revolt against Hashem should not only be removed from the *reshut harabim* — public area — so that they are no longer disseminating their anti-Torah views. They, too, must come into the *reshut hayachid* — private domain of Hashem — and become authentic Torah observing Jews.

(התוועדיות תשמ״ח ח״ב ע׳ 124, 688 – עמק המלך שער קרית ארבע (ק״ח,א) קהלת יעקב ערך תרמוד)

"מצוותה עד שתכלה הרגל מן השוק"

"The commandment of *Chanukah* lights extends until the passersby have vanished from the market." (*Shabbat* 21b)

QUESTION: Why did the *Gemara* use an obscure way of measuring the time? Why not simply say "until ½ hour after nightfall?"

ANSWER: The terminology concerning the *halachah* can be explained as a metaphor conveying an important insight:

It is common for people to work during the day to earn a livelihood. However, some unfortunately, are so engaged in materialism that they "moonlight" on another job and work nights to reach their financial goals. Often this pseudo-success is at the cost of their Torah learning, *davening* with a *minyan*, etc.

It was the goal of the Syrian-Greeks to cause the Jews to forget Torah and to cease the observance of Hashem's statutes.

The miracle with the flask of oil and the kindling of the *Menorah* emphasizes the importance of Torah study and *mitzvot* performance. The candles of the *Menorah* and the light it emanates represent Torah and *mitzvot*, as King Shlomo says "For the candle is a *mitzvah* and Torah is light" (Proverbs 6:23). The *Gemara* (*Megillah* 16b) says that *"orah"* — "light"

— means Torah. The pure oil miraculously found is also a hint to Torah, as the *Gemara* (*Berachot* 57a) says, "One who sees olive oil in a dream can anticipate receiving the light of Torah."

The *halachah* conveys the message that one can be said to have properly fulfilled the essence of *Chanukah* only when he comes to the realization that *"tichleh regel min hashuk"* — his "foot" should not be roaming around in the evening in the marketplace seeking opportunities for material gain; rather after a day's work his feet should be leading him in the direction of the *shul* and *Beit Midrash* to study Torah and pray with a *minyan*.

One should always remember that excessive involvement in business does not make one successful. Rather Hashem is the one who provides each of us with our "flask of oil," and success can come miraculously without working tirelessly day and night.

(פון אונזער אלטען אוצר בשם ר' משה ליב זצ"ל מ'סאסוב)

*   *   *

A *chasid* of Rabbi Sholom DovBer Schneersohn (the fifth Lubavitcher Rebbe), went into the business of producing overshoes. It was soon apparent that his mind was more preoccupied with business matters than the observance of Torah and *mitzvot*. Once, when he visited Lubavitch, the Rebbe said to him, "Feet enveloped in overshoes are commonplace, but imagine a 'head' sunk in overshoes!"

"כבתה אין זקוק לה"

"If the *Chanukah* lights became extinguished, one is not obliged to rekindle it." (*Shabbat* 21b)

QUESTION: The kindling of the *Chanukah* lights commemorates the miracle of the Hasmonean's candle lighting in the *Beit Hamikdash* and is the main *mitzvah* of the festival; Wouldn't it be logical that one should be obligated to rekindle any of the lights which are extinguished?

ANSWER: The Syrian-Greeks' primary intent was to abolish the study of Torah so that Jews and non-Jews alike should engage only in secular studies.

With the *halachah* concerning the extinguishing of the light the Sages are conveying a very important lesson regarding the superiority of Torah study over all secular studies.

When a person studies a secular subject for a period of time and afterwards realizes that his comprehension was faulty, or the conclusion he sought to derive from his theories on the subject matter is incorrect and unfounded, he is greatly disappointed and considers his time wasted.

Torah study, however, is not the same. If one spends much time trying to comprehend a piece of *Gemara* and in the end cannot figure it out, or if one tries to draw certain conclusions from a Torah subject and afterwards realizes that he erred, the time spent is not wasted, and he receives Heavenly reward for the *mitzvah* of *Talmud Torah* — his studying of Torah.

Celebrating *Chanukah* with the kindling of lights, emphasizes the importance of Torah study, which is compared to light. This *halachah* about the light teaches us that if one studied Torah diligently and at the end it extinguished — i.e. he didn't properly understand it or was in error — the rule is not that he receives no reward till he rekindles it, i.e. studies the subject again and comprehends it properly — rather he gets Heavenly reward for all his time and effort.

The reward for secular knowledge comes from humans, and they give recognition only for accomplishment. Hashem's reward for Torah study is primarily for the effort and toil and not for accomplishment. There is a popular saying, *"Kudsha B'rich Hu chadi b'pipula d'oraita"* — "Hashem rejoices when he sees people engaged in arguing and discussing Torah subjects," regardless of the conclusions or whether the theories are right or wrong.

(בני יששכר)

* * *

In the prayer recited after completing a *Gemara*, we say that the advantage of Torah learners over those involved in worldly matters is that "We toil and they toil. We toil and receive reward and they toil and do not receive reward." (See *Berachot* 28b.) This is problematic because every employee usually receives some sort of payment.

The superior reward for Torah can be illustrated with the following parable: In a big company there are many employees, from the chief executive officer to the blue collar workers on the assembly line. Usually the chief executive officer receives a large salary, and the blue collar worker often only gets minimum wage. While the blue collar employee on the assembly line puts in a full day with sweat and toil, the chief executive officer is often away on vacation or having a leisurely business lunch.

One may reflect on the injustice of it all: The dedicated employee should receive the generous salary while the chief executive officer should receive nominal compensation for his leisurely work. However, the fact is that the world recognizes and rewards accomplishment, not effort.

G-d's system of reward is the reverse. If one learns a piece of *Gemara* quickly and easily, he receives a smaller reward than one who spends much time and struggles with it. Thus, the famed adage: "G-d does not count the folio pages, but the hours spent studying."

"הדלקה עושה מצוה לפיכך אם כבתה קודם זמנה אין זקוק לה"

"The kindling principally accomplishes the *mitzvah* of *Chanukah* light, therefore, if it became prematurely extinguished, one is not obliged to rekindle it." (*Shulchan Aruch, Orach Chaim* 673:2)

QUESTION: What lesson can one apply to his service of Hashem from this *halachah*?

ANSWER: Many people have a tendency to refrain from undertaking something if they don't envision themselves completing it or if they question their chances for success.

Thus, they will not sit down to learn if they don't have enough time to complete the subject.

This *halachah* teaches that this is an erroneous approach. It is the obligation of the Jew to do, and it is not the Jew's obligation to accomplish. Hashem does not expect of us guaranteed success; this is up to Him. We must do our best; He will do the rest.

One must always bear in mind that *"hadlakah oseh mitzvah"* — principally, the kindling accomplishes the *mitzvah* of *Chanukah* — it is for us to make a concerted effort to accomplish; what happens afterwards is not our concern.

There is a popular saying: *"Adam oseh b'yadav v'Hashem mevareich ma'asei yadav"* — "Man should do with his hands, and Hashem will bless the work of his hands."

"שמן זית מצוה מן המובחר"

"Olive oil is the most preferable"
(*Orach Chaim* 673:1)

QUESTION: Why is olive oil the most preferable for *Chanukah* candle lighting?

ANSWER: The *Midrash* (*Shemot Rabbah* 36:1) says that the Jewish people may be compared to [olive] oil. Unlike all other liquids, which mix very well one with another, oil does not. It forever maintains its identity and will ultimately float on the top. Likewise, all the nations of the worlds mix with one another through intermarriage, and the Jews are forbidden to intermarry or assimilate with other nations.

According to the *Gemara* (*Menachot* 53b) Jews are compared to olive oil, because just as the olive gives its oil only after it is crushed and beaten, likewise, when Jews are, G-d forbid, crushed and beaten, they do *Teshuvah* — repent — and their real glory comes to bear.

Thanks to the devoted Jews who refused to assimilate and accept the Greek ideology, Hashem brought about the salvation. Since they maintained their separateness, similar to oil, and went through an excruciating struggle for Torah and *mitzvot*, like the olive, Hashem made the miracle with the olive oil. To commemorate this we prefer to use olive oil for kindling the *Chanukah Menorah*.

* * *

In the book of Lamentations (1:3) the prophet Yirmeyahu says *"Kol rodefehah hisuguhah bein hametzarim"* — "All her pursuers overtook her in narrow straits." A Chassidic Rabbi, explained that *"hisuguhah"* — "overtook her" — comes from the word *"hasagah"* — understanding and comprehending. Those who pursue the Jews don't really have an insight as to what a Jew really is and the inherent inner strength and conviction he possesses. However, all those who pursue the Jews, *hisuguhah* — get an understanding of what a Jew really is — at the time when the Jew is *bein hametzarim* — in difficult straits. The inner beauty of the Jew comes to surface and he prays earnestly for Hashem's salvation. The gentile world is amazed when they behold that in troublesome times Jews cling tenaciously to their faith and will refuse to be detached from Hashem.

(ר' נפתלי זצ"ל מראפשיטץ)

* * *

There are some Jews who profess to be atheists. This is, however, only superficial, and in difficult times when they are being "crushed" their inner beauty comes to surface.

The Lubavitcher Rebbe told a story which he heard from his father-in-law, the previous Lubavitcher Rebbe, Rabbi Yosef Yitzchak Schneersohn. The Previous Rebbe related that when bombs fell on Warsaw, people ran to hide. One time a large group was gathered together: the *Rebbe*, average people, simple folk, and some who had thought that they had nothing to do with *Yiddishkeit*. When a bomb exploded close by, *all* of them together cried out *"Shema Yisrael.."*!

It is difficult to attain something that will touch the soul-aspect of *Yechidah*, the very core of the soul. But when this does happen, whether under dire circumstances or in a pleasant way, even the lowliest and least worthy will cry out *"Shema Yisrael"* with the same intensity as the very leader of Israel.

(לקוטי שיחות ח"ב פ' חוקת)

"נר חנוכה מצוה להניחה על פתח ביתו מבחוץ ...
ובשעת הסכנה מניחה על השלחן ודיו"

"The requirement is to place the *Chanukah* light by the outside door of one's house ... and in a time of danger he should place it on his table, that is sufficient to fulfill the *mitzvah*." (Shabbat 21b)

QUESTION: What message does this *halachah* convey?

ANSWER: The word *Chanukah* is from the Hebrew word *"chinuch"* — *"education."* The message of *Chanukah* is that one must go out into the street and illuminate its darkness. In other words, one must go out and educate the masses who are alienated to Torah and *mitzvot*. Simultaneously, a person should never forget about his obligation to educate and inculcate his own children with a love of Torah and *mitzvot*.

The *halachah* teaches us that even if it is a time of "danger" and one is unable to propagate Torah and *Yiddishkeit* publicly, he must nevertheless put the *Chanukah* light on his own table; i.e. he is never exempt from teaching his own children and family, imbuing them to live a Torah-true way of life, regardless of the difficulties or risks.

(פון אונזער אלטען אוצר בשם עוללות אפרים)

"נר חנוכה שהניחה למעלה מעשרים אמה פסולה"

"A *Chanukah* light which is placed higher than 20 cubits is invalid."

QUESTION: What is the significance of the number 20 in this law?

ANSWER: This *halachah* can be interpreted as a metaphor for the following:

In the Torah Hashem gave us 613 positive and negative commandments. In addition, over the years, the Rabbis added another seven making it a total of 620 *mitzvot*. In the *Aseret Hadibrot* — Ten Commandments (*Shemot* 20:2-14) — there are a total of 620 letters. Each letter represents one of the 613 Torah *mitzvot* and the last two words *"asher lerei'acha"* (אשר לרעך), which have seven letters, represent the seven *mitzvot* instituted by Rabbinic ordinance.

They are as follows:

א = אבילות, the laws of mourning.

ש = שמחת חתן וכלה, the seven days of celebration for a groom and bride.

ר = רחיצה, the laws of *nitilat yadayim* — washing of hands before a meal.

ל = לחם, the laws of saying a *berachah* before eating food and also that breads and foods baked or cooked by gentiles are forbidden to us, even if there is no problem about the *kashrut* of the ingredients.

ר = רשויות, the laws added by the Rabbis regarding domains where it is forbidden to carry on *Shabbat*, and also the distance permissible to walk out of residential area on *Shabbat*.

ע = עמלק, the laws pertaining to reading the *Megillah* on *Purim*, and the other *mitzvot* of *Purim* — Haman was a descendant of Amalek, and *Purim* commemorates the victory over him.

ך = כהנים, celebrating *Chanukah* with kindling the *Menorah* and reciting *Hallel* to commemorate the miracle of *Chanukah*, which was brought about through the *Kohanim* of the family of Matityahu.

The number 620 is also the numerical value of the word *"keter"* (כתר) — "crown" — and the 620 *mitzvot* are Hashem's crown of glory. The Hebrew word *"esrim"* (עשרים) — "twenty" — numerically also adds up to 620.

To dispel the erroneous thought that some may have that *Chanukah* is not a *mitzvah,* but rather it is a national and social celebration, the Sages tell us in an allegoric way that placing a *Chanukah* candelabra "above *esrim*" (620) — i.e. to claim that it is not part of the 620 *mitzvot* which are part of Hashem's "crown" — is celebrating *Chanukah* in a disqualified fashion.

(בני יששכר)

"וְאִם הָיָה דָּר בַּעֲלִיָּיה מַנִּיחָהּ בַּחַלּוֹן הַסְּמוּכָה לִרְשׁוּת הָרַבִּים"

"If one lives on an upper floor, he should place the light inside his house by a window that faces the street." (*Shabbat* 21b)

QUESTION: *"Aliyah"* literally means an "attic." Since this *halachah* applies to all upper floors, it should have said *"komah gevohah"*?

ANSWER: This *halachah* may be interpreted as an allegory: The laws of *Chanukah* teach us that one must go out and illuminate the "street" with the knowledge of Torah and G-dliness. There are people, however, who consider themselves too prominent to get involved with unlearned or unaffiliated Jews. The *Gemara* (*Sukkah* 45b) describes some people as *"B'nei aliyah"* — "people of ascent" (i.e. they have reached the highest level of prominence).

Thus, the message of this *halachah* is that one may live in an *"aliyah"* — he may be a very prominent person and it may, in his opinion, be below his dignity to be involved with common-folk. Nevertheless, he may not close himself up in his "ivory tower"; rather, he must make provisions that the holiness radiating in his home should influence the public domain.

(לקוטי שיחות ח"כ ע' 634)

"פְּתִילוֹת וּשְׁמָנִים שֶׁאָמְרוּ חֲכָמִים אֵין מַדְלִיקִין בָּהֶם בְּשַׁבָּת מַדְלִיקִין בָּהֶם בַּחֲנוּכָה"

"[Concerning] wicks and oils of which the Sages said, 'We may not kindle with them on

the *Shabbat*,' we may, however, kindle with
them on *Chanukah*." (*Shabbat* 21b)

QUESTION: Why is candle lighting on *Chanukah* treated
with more leniency than on *Shabbat?*

ANSWER: Strangely, many people who do not observe
the lighting of *Shabbat* candles, nevertheless, do kindle the
Chanukah Menorah. How can this be explained?

According to the *Zohar* (III, 187a) the *petilah* — wick — is
an allusion to the Jewish body. The oil is an allusion to
mitzvot — good deeds. The *Shechinah* is compared to the flame
of a lamp. The *Shechinah* does not rest on a man's body, which
is likened to a wick, except through good deeds alone, and it
is not sufficient that his *neshamah* — soul — which is part of
G-dliness from Above, should act for him as oil to the wick.
(See *Likkutei Amarim, Tanya,* ch. 35.)

This *halachah* teaches an important lesson regarding the
strong influence that emanates from the *Chanukah* lights. Our
Sages have said that *petilot* — the wicks — i.e. people who are
not inspired by the *mitzvah* (oil) of kindling *Shabbat* candles,
and thus avoid its performance, nevertheless may be inspired
to kindle *Chanukah* candles. This *mitzvah* causes an awakening
in them that they are members of Hashem's chosen people.

(ר' מנחם מענדל זצ"ל מקוצק)

Perhaps this is a reason why the Lubavitcher Rebbe made
such an effort for public *Chanukah* candle lighting and
established a campaign that Jews of all walks of life regardless
of affiliation or commitment should kindle *Chanukah* lights.

"נר חנוכה משמאל מזוזה מימין"

**"The *Chanukah* light shall be on the left
and the *mezuzah* on the right." (*Shabbat* 22a)**

QUESTION: Why mention at all about the *mezuzah* — the
main thing we need to know is that the *Chanukah* light should
be on the right side of the doorway?

ANSWER: According to *Midrash Chanukah,* because the Jews lacked in proper observance of *mezuzah,* the Syrian-Greeks decreed that the Jews remove the doors to their tents so that they should not be able to hide within the confines of their homes and perform *mitzvot.* This imposed upon the Jews the hardship of living a few years lacking privacy.

When the Jews were victorious over their enemies, they replaced the doors to their tents and also corrected the previous laxness in the *mitzvah* of *mezuzah.* Therefore, the Rabbis ordained that we should place the *Chanukah* light at the doors to our homes opposite the *mezuzah,* to emphasize our gain thanks to Hashem's salvations and also to emphasize that our doorways have *mezuzot.*

(נר מצוה, ועי׳ אגרת השמד להרמב״ם פ״ב)

"נר חנוכה מצוה להניחה על פתח ביתו מבחוץ"

"The requirement is to place the *Chanukah* light by the doorway of one's house from the outside." (*Shabbat* 21b)

QUESTION: What is the significance of placing the *Menorah* at the entrance of one's doorway to the street?

ANSWER: *Chanukah* is a preparation for the Messianic Age, when we will go out of *galut* — exile — and enjoy the most glorious time destined for the Jewish people (see p. 17). Placing the *Chanukah Menorah* by the doorway of one's house from the outside is an expression of our eagerness and anticipation for the time when we will "go out" of *galut* under the leadership of King *Mashiach.*

"אמר רב הונא הרגיל בנר הויין ליה בנים תלמידי חכמים"

"Rav Huna said, "One who is habitual in kindling the [*Chanukah*] light will have sons who are Torah scholars." (*Shabbat* 23b)

QUESTION: Instead of *"haragil"* — "one who is habitual" — it should have said *"hamadlik"* — "one who kindles"?

ANSWER: There are many Jews, who are meticulously Torah observant in the confines of their home, but who are afraid or ashamed to openly practice a Torah life in public. When they come among society, they do not proudly demonstrate that their lifestyle is in accordance with authentic Torah teaching.

The slogan of the early Reform movement in Germany was *"Yehudi beveitecha ve'adam betzeitecha"* — "Be a true Jew at home, but on the outside be a person like everyone else." Similarly, Korach said of the Jewish people *"Kol ha'eida kulam kedoshim"* — "The entire community is holy" — *"uvetocham Hashem"* — "and G-d is among them" (*Bamidbar* 16:3). He meant that the Jews were all holy since they all had G-d *"betocham"* — "in their hearts." He asserted, thus, that it is sufficient to be a good Jew on the "inside" without openly showing it on the outside.

The *halachah* regarding the kindling of the *Chanukah* lights is that it should be done "by the doorway of one's house from the outside" so that the lights will be visible to the passersby on the street. Candles and lights are analogous to Torah and *mitzvot*, as King Shlomo said "For a candle is a *mitzvah* and Torah is light" (Proverbs 6:23). Hence, the message of *Chanukah* kindling is that a Jew should not only follow the ways of Torah and *mitzvot* in his house, but rather proudly demonstrate on the outside in front of all passersby that he is proud to be a Jew who performs Hashem's *mitzvot*.

"Haragil beneir" — "One who is habitual in kindling the [Chanukah] light" — means that the message of the *Chanukah* light has become an integral part of a Jew's conduct and throughout the *entire* year he proudly portrays his allegiance to Hashem and love for Torah and *mitzvot*. When children see that their parents cherish Torah and proudly fulfill its precepts, they desire to know more about the things that mean so much to their parents. They eagerly study Torah, and this studying will ultimately make them into *Talmidei Chachamim* — Torah scholars.

(נרות שמונה)

"וצריכין להניחו (השמש) קצת למעלה מן הנרות
שיהא ניכר שאינו ממנין הנרות"

"The shamash should be placed a little higher than the other lights, in order that it may be obvious that it is not one of the required number of candles. (*Kitzur Shulchan Aruch* 139:14, *Maharil*)

QUESTION: Where is there a hint in Torah that the *shamash* should be placed *higher* than the other candles?

ANSWER: There is an expression in (Isaiah 6:2) *"Serafim omdim mema'al lo."* The word *"lo"* (לו) has the numerical value of 36, which is the total number of candles lit during the eight days of *Chanukah*. *"Serafim"* means "the fiery ones," a reference" that the *shamashim* that kindle the candles — *"mema'al"* — should be placed above — *"lo"* — the 36 candles.

(מהרי"ל)

* * *

A very important lesson can be learned from the *shamash*, which stands as a servant above all the other candles and yet doesn't count in the number of candles. The *shamash* coaxes all the candles to life and then stands watch over them, lest one falter and require a fresh boost of light. It is an imparter of light to others, but it never attains the station of a *Chanukah* light in its own right.

Yet despite — indeed because of — this, the *shamash* towers above all the other lights of the *Menorah*, because there is no greater virtue than to forgo one's own luminary potential in order to awaken a flame in others.

תפילות
Prayers

ORDER OF KINDLING THE *CHANUKAH* LIGHTS — *BERACHOT*
HANEIROT HALLALU
MEHADRIN MIN HAMEHADRIN
MAOZ TZUR
AL HANISSIM

ברכות

בָּרוּךְ אַתָּה יְיָ אֱלֹהֵינוּ מֶלֶךְ הָעוֹלָם, אֲשֶׁר קִדְּשָׁנוּ בְּמִצְוֹתָיו, וְצִוָּנוּ לְהַדְלִיק נֵר, חֲנֻכָּה:

בָּרוּךְ אַתָּה יְיָ אֱלֹהֵינוּ מֶלֶךְ הָעוֹלָם, שֶׁעָשָׂה נִסִּים לַאֲבוֹתֵינוּ בַּיָּמִים הָהֵם בִּזְמַן הַזֶּה:

בָּרוּךְ אַתָּה יְיָ אֱלֹהֵינוּ מֶלֶךְ הָעוֹלָם, שֶׁהֶחֱיָנוּ וְקִיְּמָנוּ וְהִגִּיעָנוּ לִזְמַן הַזֶּה:

"בָּרוּךְ... לְהַדְלִיק נֵר חֲנֻכָּה"

"Blessed... to kindle the *Chanukah* light."

QUESTION: On *Shabbat* all make the *Berachah* "lehadlik neir *shel* Shabbat" — "to kindle the light *of* Shabbat." Why don't all say *"shel Chanukah"* — *"of Chanukah"*?

ANSWER: The *Chanukah* candles are considered holy and therefore are not to be used for any personal pleasure or for illumination. On the other hand, the *Shabbat* candles are for the purpose of illuminating the home. They assure that *shalom bayit* — peace in the home — prevail. Thanks to the home being illuminated, one will avoid tripping over obstacles and getting into arguments over who is to blame. Eating the *Shabbat* meal in a luminous area enhances ones *oneg* — delight — of *Shabbat* (*Shulchan Aruch HaRav* 263:1). The expression *"neir Chanukah,"* without the word *"shel"* — "of" — subtly implies total consecration to the *mitzvah* of *Chanukah*, and that it may not be used for any other purpose.

Saying *"neir shel Shabbat"* implies that the light also has an independent purpose of its own and is not consecrated. True, they are lit in honor of the *Shabbat,* but they are also lit so that the additional light they produce in the room can be used by the inhabitants to enhance their pleasure and thus experience a delightful *Shabbat.*

(ברכי יוסף תרע"ו)

Order of Kindling the Chanukah Lights

On the first night the three following blessings are recited; on the subsequent seven nights, the third blessing, *Shehechiyanu* is omitted. The lights are kindled only *after* all the blessings are recited.

On the first night, we light the candle to the extreme right of the *Menorah*. On each night, a new candle is added to the left of the previous night's lights. The newest light is always kindled first, the one to the right second, and so on.

Blessed are You, *A-donai*, our God, King of the universe, Who has sanctified us with His commandments, and commanded us to kindle the *Chanukah* light.

Blessed are You, *A-donai*, our God, King of the universe, Who performed miracles for our forefathers in those days, at this time.

The following blessing is recited on the first day. **Blessed are you, *A-donai*, our God, King of the universe, Who has granted us life, sustained us and enabled us to reach this occasion.**

Alternatively, the kindling of the *Chanukah* candles is the only tangible act done in celebrating *Chanukah*. The lighting of the *Shabbat* candles, however, is only one of many practices which are done in connection with celebrating *Shabbat* (e.g. *Kiddush*, *Shabbat* meal, etc.). Hence, by saying *"neir Chanukah"* (without *"shel"*), we are accentuating that *"neir"* — "candle" — is the essence and only action of *Chanukah*. On *Shabbat*, however, one adds the word *"shel"* because the candle is not the only dimension and essence of the *Shabbat;* rather it is one aspect among the many, aspects *of Shabbat*.

(מחזיק ברכה לחיד״א הובא בשערי תשובה, תרע״ו)

"בָּרוּךְ... לְהַדְלִיק נֵר חֲנוּכָּה"

"Blessed... to kindle the *Chanukah* light."

QUESTION: What message does the wording of the *Berachah* impart when the word *"shel"* is omitted?

ANSWER: The *Arizal* writes in his *siddur* that during *Chanukah* the thirteen attributes of mercy *"mei'irin"* — radiate. Each day one of the thirteen shines and on the eighth day — *Zot Chanukah* — the balance from *notzer chesed* — Preserver of Kindness — until *venakeih lo yenakeai* — Who Absolves, but does not absolve completely — shine.

When we omit the word *"shel"* from the *berachah* pronounced for the candle lighting, the *berachah* contains thirteen words, corresponding to the 13 attributes of mercy that shine during *Chanukah*.

(שם משמואל)

* * *

Incidentally, the second *berachah* of *"she'asah nisim"* which is recited every night of *Chanukah* also consists of thirteen words. Thus, the two *berachot* together have a total of 26 words. The holy four letter Name, the Tetragramaton (י-ה-ו-ה), also has the numerical value of 26 and connotes His mercy. With the 26 words in the two *berachot* we are indicating that all the events of *Chanukah* were thanks to His mercy for his dedicated servants and we thank Him profusely for it.

(כף החיים סי' תרע"ו בשם קב הישר)

* * *

Alternatively, on *Chanukah* we light thirty six candles and eight *shamashim*, a total of forty four candles. Since the *Zohar* (1:77b) says that when there is an *itaruta deletata* — an awakening from below — it evokes an *itaruta dele'eila* — an awakening above, Hashem also, so to speak, kindles forty four candles during *Chanukah*, bringing the total candles lit to eighty eight. The first letters of the words *"lehadlik neir*

Chanukah" (להדליק נר חנוכה) add up to 88 to allude to this concept.

* * *

The first letters of the words *"lehadlik neir Chanukah"* (ל׳ נ׳ ח׳) are also the first letters of the words *"nafsheinu chiktah L'Hashem"* (נפשינו חכתה לי-ה-ו-ה) — "our soul longed to Hashem [He is our help and our shield]" (Psalms 33:20). Because of our devotion and longing to Hashem we merited that *"hapach* (פח) *nishbar"* — "[the hunters] snare broke" — i.e. the kingdom of Antiochus was broken, *"ve'anachnu nimlatnu"* — "and we escaped" (Ibid 124:7). In commemoration, below on earth and above in heaven, *pach* (פח) — 88 — candles are kindled.

(קדושת לוי בדרושים לחנוכה בשם האריז״ל)

"ברוך... להדליק נר חנוכה"
"Blessed... to kindle the *Chanukah* light."

QUESTION: Why isn't the wording of the *berachah*, *"Lehadlik neir shel Chanukah?"*

Answer: During the *Chanukah* candle lighting Hashem reveals a radiance in the world which resembles the great radiance the world will enjoy in the *Messianic* era. The words *"lehadlik neir Chanukah"* (להדליק נר חנוכה) numerically add up to 518 and *im hakolel* — counting the statement as one — adds up to 519, as do the words *"ohr chodosh"* (אור חדש) — new light.

The *berachah* was authored without the word *"shel,"* so that its words would be equivalent to *"ohr chodosh."* This is an allusion that on *Chanukah*, during the candle lighting, Hashem reveals in the world a semblance of the "new light" which will shine when *Mashiach* comes.

The reason the words *"lehadlik neir Chanukah"* themselves have a slightly lower numerical value than the words *"ohr chodosh,"* is that what is now revealed is only a *"me'ein"* — a radiance derived from the light to be revealed in the future, but not the full brilliance that will exist then.

(בני יששכר)

"ברוך... להדליק נר חנוכה"

"Blessed... to kindle the *Chanukah* light."

QUESTION: Instead of saying *"lehadlik"* — to kindle — why don't we say *"al hadlakat neir Chanukah"* — *"concerning the kindling of Chanukah* light" — similar to the blessing for a circumcision, *"al hamilah"* — "concerning the circumcision"?

ANSWER: There are certain *mitzvot* that one must perform personally and for which one cannot appoint a *sheliach* — emissary — to perform it on his behalf. For these *mitzvot* the *berachah* is said with a *lamed*, as in the case of *tefillin*: *"lehaniach tefillin."* Since the father can appoint an emissary to circumcise his son and since the father is not required to personally circumcise his son or to even be present physically at the circumcision, the *berachah* is *"al hamilah."*

It is true that not every member of the household must kindle his own *Chanukah* candles and if one is away from home, he can be *yotzi* — fulfill the *mitzvah* — with the host's candle lighting. Nevertheless, since everyone must be personally present at the candle lighting and it is popular custom that every person lights candles in his own home to demonstrate his love to Hashem for the miracle He performed on our behalf, lighting the *Menorah* is therefore in the category of *mitzvot* which the doer performs alone. Therefore the *berachah* is with a *lamed* (*lehadlik*) the same as for *mitzvot* which one cannot delegate to others.

Alternatively, even if one is relying on his host's candlelighting he must contribute towards the cost of the oil or candles. Thus, *Chanukah* candle kindling is considered a *mitzvah shebegufo* — one which must be performed personally and which cannot be delegated to an emissary and therefore the *berachah* is *"lehadlik"* with a *lamed*.

(ריב"א הובא ברא"ש על פסחים פרק ראשון ור"ן הובא שם בקרבן נתנאל)

"בָּרוּךְ אַתָּה ... לְהַדְלִיק נֵר חֲנוּכָּה, שֶׁעָשָׂה נִסִּים, שֶׁהֶחֱיָנוּ..."

"Blessed are You ... to kindle the *Chanukah* light. Who performed miracles, Who has kept us alive."

QUESTION: Where is there a *remez* — hint — in the Torah for the three blessings recited on the first night of *Chanukah,* when one kindles the *Menorah?*

ANSWER: When the people spoke against Hashem and Moshe regarding the redemption from Egypt and the manna, they were bitten by fiery snakes as a punishment. When the people expressed remorse, Hashem instructed Moshe, "Make a burning one [fiery serpent] and place it in a pole and it will be that anyone who had been bitten will look at it and live" (*Bamidbar* 21:8).

This entire *pasuk* is a hint for the three *berachot;* "*Asei lecha saraf*" — "make a burning one [fiery serpent]" — corresponds to the *berachah* of *lehadlik neir Chanukah* — to kindle the *Chanukah* light."

"*Vesim oto al neis*" — "place it upon a *neis*" — corresponds to the second *berachah* of *she'asah nissim* — Who performed miracles.

"*Vachai*" — "and live" — corresponds to the third *berachah* of *Shehechiyanu* — who kept us alive.

(מטה משה סי' תתק"פ)

הנרות הללו

הַנֵּרוֹת הַלָּלוּ אָנוּ מַדְלִיקִין, עַל הַתְּשׁוּעוֹת, וְעַל הַנִּסִּים, וְעַל
הַנִּפְלָאוֹת, שֶׁעָשִׂיתָ לַאֲבוֹתֵינוּ בַּיָּמִים הָהֵם בִּזְּמַן הַזֶּה, עַל יְדֵי
כֹּהֲנֶיךָ הַקְּדוֹשִׁים. וְכָל שְׁמוֹנַת יְמֵי חֲנֻכָּה, הַנֵּרוֹת הַלָּלוּ קֹדֶשׁ הֵם,
וְאֵין לָנוּ רְשׁוּת לְהִשְׁתַּמֵּשׁ בָּהֶן, אֶלָּא לִרְאוֹתָן בִּלְבָד, כְּדֵי לְהוֹדוֹת
וּלְהַלֵּל לְשִׁמְךָ הַגָּדוֹל, עַל נִסֶּיךָ וְעַל נִפְלְאוֹתֶיךָ, וְעַל יְשׁוּעוֹתֶיךָ:

"הנרות הללו"

"These lights."

QUESTION: The words *"Haneirot Halallu"* — "these lights" — are plural. On the first night when we only kindle one light, shouldn't we say *"haneir hazeh"* — "this light?"

ANSWER: When a Jew performs a *mitzvah* on earth he evokes a spiritual awakening in heaven, and Hashem, so to speak, also performs the *mitzvah*. This is the concept of *"itaruta deletata itaruta deli'eilah"* — "the awakening below causes an awakening above." Thus when we kindle *Chanukah* lights, Hashem also does so in heaven (see p. 72). Hence, on the first night two lights are really being lit and the expression *Haneirot Halallu* — these lights — in plural is in proper order.

"הנרות הללו אנו מדליקין על התשועות ועל הנסים ועל הנפלאות
שעשית לאבותינו בימים ההם... להודות ולהלל לשמך הגדול
על נסיך ועל נפלאותיך ועל ישועותיך."

"These lights we kindle upon the salvations, miracles and wonders which You performed for our forefathers... to express thanks and praise to Your great name for the miracles, wonders and salvations."

QUESTION: Why in the beginning is the order "salvations, miracles and wonders" while in the conclusion of the prayer the order is "miracles, wonders and salvations"?

Haneirot Hallalu

After one light has been lit, say *Haneirot Hallalu* while continuing to light the others. The *Chabad* custom is to recite *Haneirot Hallalu* after *all* the candles are lit.

We kindle these lights [to commemorate] the salvations, miracles and wonders which You have performed for our forefathers, in those days at this time, through Your holy *Kohanim*. Throughout the eight days of *Chanukah*, these lights are sacred, and we are not permitted to make use of them, but only to look at them, in order to offer thanks and praise to Your great Name for Your miracles, for Your wonders and for Your salvations.

ANSWER: These three terms are not merely descriptive terms relating to a given event; rather each is a distinct way to accurately categorize the uniqueness of what happened.

"Salvation" (תשועות) means, for example, that when a group is at war against another group, and it appears that one side was victorious because of their superior strategy or tactics, in reality it is Hashem that brought about their salvation, and without His assistance and salvation no one can ever succeed.

"Miracles" (נסים) are occurrences that are above and beyond the worldly laws of nature, such as a victory of the weak over the strong or the few over the many.

"Wonders" (נפלאות) are happenings that arouse people's amazement and bring about a state of wonderment. Though a wonder can be explained by some as not being an actual miracle, nevertheless, it is not something that one would normally anticipate and people view it with awe and astonishment.

In the beginning of *Haneirot Hallalu* we speak of what Hashem did for our forefathers in *those* days. A careful analysis of the history as recorded by Yossifus — Josephus —

will show that in the beginning the victories the Jews experienced were not miracles but merely acts attributed to Hashem's salvation. Afterwards, they literally saw not just His salvation but *nissim* — miracles — miraculous success, followed by *nifla'ot* — acts of wonder.

Matityahu and his sons fought the Syrian-Greeks and the Hellenite Jews for three years. They started their battles while they lived in Modi'in — a Judean village located approximately 10 miles from Jerusalem.

One day the king's forces appeared and demanded that the townspeople offer a sacrifice in the pagan fashion. They attempted to convince the aged and venerable Matityahu that it would be to his material and social advantage if he would set an example for the people. Were he to comply, he and his sons would be considered the king's "friends," an official title carrying with it many privileges, and they would receive a handsome monetary reward. Matityahu proudly and publicly declared his determination to remain faithful to the religion of his forefathers. As he was declaiming his defiance, a renegade Jew approached the altar to offer a pig as a sacrifice. When Matityahu saw this, he grabbed a sword and killed not only the Jewish renegade, but the Syrian emissaries of the king.

Thereupon, he and his sons left all their worldly possessions in Modi'in and fled to the mountains in the Judean desert. Many other loyal Jews followed his example and joined him to live in the mountain caves, where they would be able to practice the Torah's precepts. The king's forces could not disregard this challenge to their authority and began to seek out these bands of loyal Jews in the mountains. The Jews were exhorted by Matityahu to resist the Greeks with force, and six thousand combat-worthy, loyal Jews gathered under his banner. They began to strike back at the Greeks and demolish the idolatrous altars put up by the pagans.

In these early stages of confrontation, the victories the Jews experienced were not miracles. The victory of a group of Jews fighting a band of Hellenists is not anything unusual, but it was indeed thanks to Hashem's *Teshu'a* — salvation.

As time progressed and Antiochus learned about the defeats his troops were encountering, he became enraged and resolved to crush the Hasmoneans.

He opened his treasures and paid his soldiers a full year's wages in advance and ordered them to prepare for combat. Antiochus organized an army consisting of tens of thousands of footsoldiers and cavalry, equipped them with war elephants, and commanded them to march into Judea and annihilate Yehudah the Maccabbe and his small army of followers.

What followed afterwards was a great *neis* — miracle. The huge armies of the enemies were conquered by the small Jewish army divided into four segments. The weak soldiers of Judah defeated the mighty army of Antiochus.

Once this was accomplished, the Jews reclaimed the *Beit Hamikdash* and behold, they witnessed *nifla'ot* — wonders. They found a single flask of oil which the Syrian-Greeks overlooked and with it they were able to kindle the *Menorah*. The finding of the oil was not a miracle since it is not against the law of nature that a single flask which was hidden should go unnoticed, but it is indeed a wonder and people viewed it with amazement and awe. (Afterwards they witnessed another miracle, namely, that the single flask of oil lasted them miraculously for eight days — this however, is included in the plural of *"nisecha"* — *"Your miracles".*)

Hence, when talking about what our forefathers witnessed in *those* days the chronological order was *"teshu'ot"* — *"salvations"*, *"nissim"* — *"miracles"*, and *"nifla'ot"* — *"wonders."*

However, when *we* have to offer praise and thanks today, our initial reaction is to thank Him for the unbelievable *"nissim* — miracles — in which Hashem definitely changed the order of nature for our benefit. Then, after further contemplation one thanks Him for the *"nifla'ot"* — wonders — which are indeed awesome. Though some may argue that it was not so special and the oversight of the flask could have just been a haphazard occurrence, nevertheless, after careful consideration, one concludes that this is G-d's predestined wonder and we owe Him thanks for it. Ultimately, one comes to the recognition that nature too is controlled by Hashem and since *"la'Hashem hayeshuah"* — "salvation is Hashem's" — He must be thanked and praised when one experiences His salvation.

(לקוטי שיחות חט"ו ע' 366)

"הנרות הללו קדש הם"

"These lights are holy."

QUESTION: What lesson can we learn from the *Chanukah* candles?

ANSWER: 1) Candles represent Torah and *mitzvot,* as King Shlomo said, *"Neir mitzvah veTorah ohr"* — "A *mitzvah* is a candle and Torah is light (Proverbs 6:23). The additions of a candle to the *Chanukah Menorah* each day teaches that in Torah and *mitzvot,* one should never be content with what was done yesterday. Each day one must strive to do more and improve in the study of Torah and observance of *mitzvot.*

2) The *Chanukah* lights commemorate the *Menorah* of the *Beit Hamikdash.* Yet there are major differences between them. In the *Beit Hamikdash* the *Menorah* was lit in the afternoon and on the inside, whereas the *Chanukah* candles are lit by the entrance facing the street and after dark.

This teaches that a Jew must not only light up his house, as with the *Shabbat* candles, but he has the additional responsibility to illuminate the "outside" — his social and business environment.

When times are "hard" spiritually, when it is "dark" outside and the Jews are in exile, it is not sufficient to light a candle alone and maintain it; it is necessary to increase the lights steadily. Constant growing efforts to spread the light of Torah and *mitzvot* will dispel the darkness of exile and illuminate the world.

(לקוטי שיחות ח"א)

"הנרות הללו קדש הם ואין לנו רשות להשתמש בהן
אלא לראותן בלבד כדי להודות ולהלל"

"These lights are sacred, and we are not permitted to make use of them, but only to look at them in order to offer thanks and praise."

QUESTION: How does ones not being permitted to use them help us to praise Hashem?

ANSWER: If one would be permitted to use the candles for his personal benefit, he might become involved in his activities and be oblivious to the significance of the *Chanukah* candles. However, when a person must refrain from using them, and at the same time he must sit near them and look at them, all he tends to do is contemplate them and think about why they are being lit. Hence, inevitably he will begin to give thanks and praise Hashem's Holy Name.

(אדרת אליהו – ספרדי)

מהדרין מן המהדרין
The Very Scrupulous

"מצות נר חנוכה נר איש וביתו והמהדרין נר לכל אחד ואחד והמהדרין מן
המהדרין בית שמאי אומרים יום ראשון מדליק שמנה מכאן ואילך פוחת
והולך בית הלל אומרים יום ראשון מדליק אחת מכאן ואילך מוסיף והולך"

**"The basic commandment of *Chanukah* lights is for
the head of the household to light one candle for the
entire family each night. Those who want to enhance
their fulfillment of *mitzvot* light one candle each night
for each member of the household. Those who desire
to enhance their observance of *mitzvot* even further...
According to *Beit Shammai*, the first day one kindles
eight candles, and henceforth continuously decreases.
According to *Beit Hillel*, the first day one lights one
candle, and henceforth contiuously increases."**
(Shabbat 21b)

QUESTION: What exactly is the enhancement of the
mehadrin and what do the *mehadrin min hamehadrin* do?

ANSWER: According to the Rambam (*Chanukah* 4:1), the
basic *mitzvah* is that the head of the household kindle one
candle each night for the *entire* household. If he is a *mehader,*
then he is obliged to light one candle each night for each
member of his household, including females, but excluding
minors. Thus, for a family consisting of a father, mother, two
sons after *bar-mitzvah*, two daughters after *bat-mitzvah* and
one infant, the head of the household would kindle six
candles each night. According to the Rama (*Orach Chaim*
671:2), each member of the family by *himself* lights one candle
each night of *Chanukah*.

If they are *mehadrin min hamehadrin*, the Rambam rules
that according to *Beit Shammai* one continuously decreases the
amount of candles. Thus, on the first night one would kindle
eight candles for each member of his household and on the

seventh night one would kindle seven candles for each member of the household.

According to *Tosafot*, the basic *mitzvah* is one candle each night for the *entire* household. The *mehadrin* light one candle each night for every member of the household, and the *mehadrin min hamehadrin* perform the **basic** *mitzvah* of one kindling for the *entire* family in an enhanced way. Thus, according to *Beit Shammai* the head of the household lights eight candles on the first night for the *entire* family and decreases each night of the succeeding nights of *Chanukah*. According to *Beit Hillel* the head of the household lights one candle on the first night for the entire household and continuously increases the number of candles each succeeding night. Ultimately, on the eighth night, the *mehadrin min hamehadrin* kindle a total of eight candles for the *entire* household, according to *Beit Hillel*.

Hence, according to *Tosafot, mehadrin min hamehadrin* is not a third level of performance rather, another way to be *mehader* in the basic *mitzvah* of one kindling for the entire family.

It is interesting to note that the Sefardic Jews conduct themselves according to *Tosafot,* an Ashkenazic authority, and the Ashkenazic Jews conduct themselves on *Chanukah* according to the interpretation of *mehadrin min hamehadrin* of the Rambam, a *sefardi* codifier, as modified by the Rama. Hence, each member of the household lights his own *Chanukah* candles and following the opinion of *Beit Hillel,* one continuously increases the number of candles each night.

(באר היטב סי׳ תרע״א ס״ק ג, ועי׳ בהמועדים בהלכה)

"בית שמאי אומרים...פוחת והולך בית הלל אומרים...מוסיף והולך"

"According to *Beit Shammai*, the first night we light eight candles, and we decrease by one each night. According to *Beit Hillel*, the first night we light one candle, and we increase each night by one." (*Shabbat* 21b)

QUESTION: What is the basis of their dispute?

ANSWER: They are disputing which has greater significance, the *potential* (בכח) or the *actual* (בפועל). *Beit Shammai*
holds that the *potential* is more significant. The miracle of
Chanukah took place over a period of eight days. Immediately,
on the first day the oil had the *potential* to last for eight days.
Each succeeding night this *potential* was reduced; i.e. on the
first night the oil miraculously was able to last for eight, and
the second day it was able to last for seven days, etc.
Therefore, to emphasize this aspect of the miracle, we
decrease by one each night.

According to *Beit Hillel*, priority is given to the *actual* miracle. After the first night, the Jewish people witnessed a
miracle of the oil lasting one night, on the second night, they
witnessed a miracle of two nights, etc.; therefore we increase
one candle because in *actuality, the visible miracle increased* from
night to night.

(לקוטי שיחות ח"ו ע' 73)

"בית הלל אומרים יום ראשון מדליק אחת מכאן ואילך מוסיף והולך...
חד אמר טעמא דבית הלל כנגד ימים היוצאין... וחד אמר...
דמעלין בקדש ואין מורידין"

**"Beit Hillel says, 'The first night light one and
add one more each succeeding night...' One
reason is that it corresponds to the days that
passed... (another reason is that) in matters of
holiness, one should always increase
and not decrease." (Shabbat 21b)**

QUESTION: What is the *halachic* difference between the
two approaches to explain the opinion of *Beit Hillel*?

ANSWER: One difference may be as follows: When
someone possesses very limited resources, and on the second
night of *Chanukah* lights only one candle, if on the third night
he has sufficient resources, how many should he kindle?

According to those who assert that *Beit Hillel*'s opinion is
based on the days that passed, he would have to light three
candles. According to the explanation that it is necessary to

increase in holiness and not decrease, it would be sufficient to light only two candles, since the night before he lit only one.

Another difference would be in the event that on the third night of *Chanukah* one had resources sufficient only for two candles, how many should he light? If the reason for *Beit Hillel's* opinion is that it corresponds to the days that passed, the one who does not have three candles for the third night, will light only a single candle in order to fulfill the basic obligation of lighting a candle each night of *Chanukah*. According to the other explanation, one would light two candles. Although one cannot accomplish the concept of increasing in matters of holiness, at least he will not violate the command of *"ve'ein moridin"* — not to decrease in matters of holiness.

(לקוטי שיחות ח"כ)

"והמהדרין ... והמהדרין מן המהדרין"

"Those who want to enhance their fulfillment of *mitzvot*... and those who desire to enhance their observance of *mitzvot* even further..." (*Shabbat* 21b)

QUESTION: Why by *Chanukah* do we not only have *mehadrin* but also *mehadrin min hamehadrin*?

ANSWER: Halachically, the entire miracle of finding the single sealed flask of oil was superfluous. In the event that there was no undefiled oil, they could have used *tamei* oil for the *Menorah* since there is a rule that *"Tumah hutrah betzibbur"* — "tumah is permitted in regard of a community." That is, any *tumah* restriction interfering with a communal offering can be disregarded or at least *hutrah betzibbur* — overridden in regard to a community (see *Yoma* 6b).

Also, the second phase of the miracle that the single flask of oil lasted for eight days was unnecessary because technically they could have used very thin wicks so that only

1/8 of the regular amount of oil would be consumed each night.

Nevertheless, Hashem made the miracle because of his love for the Jewish people. He knew very well that they would not feel comfortable kindling the *Menorah* with defiled oil.

Knowing also that the Jews would not be happy with a much dimmer light then usual, Hashem made the miracle that enabled them to have regular wicks and thus produce a flame in its full glow for the entire eight days until a new supply of oil was available.

Consequently, because of the *two* miracles Hashem made so that we can have **two** *hiddurim* — enhancements — of the *mitzvah*, we commemorate this by kindling our *Menorah* in a way of *mehadrin min hamehadrin* — with *two* levels of embellished *mitzvah* observance.

(בית הלוי, וע׳ לקוטי שיחות ח״ל ע׳ 308)

״מצות נר חנוכה נר איש וביתו... והמהדרין מן המהדרין...
בית הלל אומרים מוסיף והולך״

"According to *halachah* it is sufficient to light one candle each night throughout *Chanukah* for the entire household. Those who are *mehadrin min hamehadrin* — extremely careful in performing *mitzvot* — follow *Beit Hillel* and add one candle each night." (*Shabbat* 21b)

QUESTION: Why, in regard to lighting the *Menorah*, do all homes conduct themselves in the manner of *mehadrin min hamehadrin* — supremely scrupulous — while in many other *mitzvot* they follow lesser *halachic* requirements?

ANSWER: In describing the miracle of *Chanukah*, the *Gemara* relates that the Jews found only one flask of oil and that it had the seal of the *Kohen Gadol*. In the *Beit Hamikdash* there were *Kohanim* assigned to the special task of making oil. It was not the responsibility of the *Kohen Gadol* to make oil. Why then did this particular flask bear the *Kohen Gadol's* seal?

The *Kohen Gadol* was required to bring a daily meal-offering consisting of flour and oil, known as *"chavitei Kohen Gadol" (Vayikra 6:15)*. Normally, the oil used for this meal-offering as well as any *karban minchah* — meal-offering, would be of lower quality than that used for the kindling of the *Menorah (Shemot 27:20, Rashi)*. However, the *Kohen Gadol* in that time was a highly distinguished spiritual personality, and a *mehader bemitzvot* — scrupulous in *mitzvot* — who used *pure* olive oil for his daily sacrifice.

When the Hasmoneans entered the *Beit Hamikdash*, they did not find any oil to kindle the *Menorah*. Luckily they found one flask which was designated for the *Kohen Gadol's* daily meal-offering, and, to their utter amazement, it was pure olive oil. Were it not for the fact that this *Kohen Gadol* was a *mehader bemitzvot*, no pure olive oil would have been available. To emphasize the uniqueness of the *Kohen Gadol* at that time, we emulate his actions in the form of *mehadrin min hamehadrin*.

(ר' אברהם מרדכי זצ"ל מגור ועי' מלא העומר)

"נשים בהדלקת נר חנוכה"

"Women and *Chanukah* kindling"

QUESTION: Why is it not the custom for the women or girls in the household to kindle their own *Menorah*?

ANSWER: The wife does not kindle because of the rule that *ishto kegufo* — the wife is considered as a part of the husband's body. Therefore when he kindles his *Menorah*, it includes her too. Since married women are not required to kindle the *Menorah*, also unmarried girls living with their parents don't kindle. Thus, the rule of doing *mitzvot* because of *chinuch* — training and practice — does not apply to girls under *Bat Mitzvah* living in their parents home.

(שו"ת שער אפרים סי' מ"ב, אליהו רבה סי' תרע"א, ועי' ספר המנהגים חב"ד ע' 69, ומשמרת שלום סי' מ"ח)

* * *

Alternatively, the Sages originally required that *Chanukah* candles be placed *"al petach beito mibachutz"* — "by the doorway of one's house, from the outside" (*Shabbat* 21b), so that they would be visible to the passersby on the street.

Based on King David's statement *"Kol kevudah bat melech penimah"* — "The very honor of a princess is within (Psalms 45:14) — the *Gemara* (*Yevamot* 76b) concludes that just as the honor and dignity of a princess requires that she remain in her palace and not go outside and mingle with the common folk, likewise, Jewish women should emulate the dignified behavior of a princess and remain in their tents.

Hence, for Jewish women to stand on the outside and kindle the *Menorah* is not compatible with modest behavior expected of them. Thus, when the *mitzvah* of kindling was first instituted and the *mehadrin* did their own kindling, the women refrained from kindling the *Menorah* by themselves and relied on the kindling done by their husbands. Consequently, they continue to do so even now if it is kindled inside the home. However, a woman living alone, has no other alternative and is obligated to kindle a *Chanukah Menorah* in her home.

(חתם סופר עמ״ס דף כ״א ע״ב ועי׳ נטעי גבריאל)

"קטן שהגיע לחינוך צריך להדליק גם כן"

"A minor who reached the stage of education must also kindle." (*Orach Chaim*, Rama 675:3)

QUESTION: How many candles should a minor kindle on each succeeding day after day one? Does he add an additional candle each night or not?

ANSWER: The *Mishnah Berurah* (675:3) writes, "Though there are opinions that he cannot be *motzi* — help others fulfill the *mitzvah* with his kindling — nevertheless, since he reached the age of education, he should light for himself. However, it appears to me that for the minor there is no need to be so stringent and only one candle each night is sufficient."

One may wonder, if so, why do all minors kindle an additional candle each night?

The *Gemara* (*Shabbat* 21b) says that through kindling one candle each night for the entire family one fulfills the *mitzvah*. However, there are *mehadrin* — those who desire to enhance their performance of Hashem's commandments in an embellished way — and *mehadrin min hamehadrin*, those who do so in an even more embellished way.

From the *pasuk* "*Zeh Keili ve'anveihu*" — "This is my G-d and I shall glorify Him (*Shemot* 15:2) — the *Gemara* (*Shabbat* 133b) derives that one is required to beautify a *mitzvah*. The *Gemara* (*Bava Kamma* 9b) explains that for the beautification of a *mitzvah* one must spend up to a third of the sum spent on the *mitzvah* itself. (For example, if one has a choice to buy one of two *etrogim*, he must spend up to one third more to buy the more beautiful one.)

In analyzing the ideas of *mehadrin* as it applies to *Chanukah*, one might wonder whether this the same idea as *hiddur mitzvah* — beautification of a *mitzvah*. If so, *Chanukah* is an exception and exceeds the rule of "up to a third" because when one lights two candles the second night the *hiddur* is actually one hundred percent. (*Rabbeinu Chananeil* — *Shabbat* 21b — draws a parallel between the two.) Or should we say that it is entirely not connected: in the case of the *etrog*, the *hiddur* — enhancement — is in the *etrog* — the *cheftza* — the item of the *mitzvah* — i.e. a nicer *etrog* as opposed to an ordinary one. In the case of *Chanukah*, however, the *hiddur* relates to the *gavra* — the person — i.e. it is another *category* of how some people fulfill the *mitzvah* of kindling the *Chanukah* lights.

A difference between these two approaches has consequences for the case of a minor. If we should say that *mehadrin* is merely a beautification of the item of the *mitzvah* per se, then one is not required when training his young son to also train him in *hiddur*. Thus, the father buys a beautiful *etrog* for himself and for his son whom he is training he suffices with teaching him the essential *mitzvah* and buys him a kosher but not *hadar etrog*. Similarly, for *Chanukah*, the father should teach the son the basic *mitzvah* of *Chanukah* candle lighting, which is that the son light one candle each night (so that when he will be a head of a household he will know the basic *mitzvah*) and he is not required to go through the expense of using more oil or candles to train him to do the *mitzvah* in an enhanced way.

Supposing we say, however, that *mehadrin* and *mehadrin min hamehadrin* of *Chanukah* is not the same concept as *hiddur mitzvah;* rather it is the method used by the people who pursue *mitzvot*. Then, it is proper for a father to teach his son to light additional candles each night so that when he becomes of age he will be a person who pursues *mitzvot*.

(עי' משנה הלכות ח"ז סי' פ"ה, ועי' לקוטי שיחות ח"כ ע' 208)

*   *   *

Alternatively, there is a question concerning one who lit seven candles on the eighth night and realized that he forgot to make the *berachah* of *"lehadlik"*: Can he still make the *berachah* before lighting the eighth candle, or do we say that one performs the basic *mitzvah* by lighting only one candle each night? (In the latter case, after the first is lit, the remainder are only considered *hiddur mitzvah* and a *berachah* is not recited over *hiddur mitzvah*.)

Regarding the *halachah* of *hiddur mitzvah* there is a *chakirah* — analytical speculation — concerning whether the *hiddur mitzvah* becomes a part of the *mitzvah*. One possibility is that it is a part of the *mitzvah* being performed but it is preferable and not obligatory, and another is that it is a separate entity. In the latter case the *mitzvah* involves the primary action, and *hiddur mitzvah* is a *mitzvah keloli* — an additional separate *halachah* that all *mitzvot* should be done *behiddur*. Thus, when doing a *mitzvah behiddur*. one fulfills two *mitzvot*: 1) the specific *mitzvah* in question and 2) the general *mitzvah* of beautifying a *mitzvah*, which is derived from *"zeh Keili ve'anveihu"* (*Shabbat* 133a).

Now if we accept the view that the *hiddur* is a part of the *mitzvah*, one would make a *berachah* even if only *hiddur* is done, since it is still part of the essential *mitzvah*. However, if it is a separate addition to the *mitzvah*, then one should not make a *berachah* because a *berachah* is made only for fulfilling the actual *mitzvah*, and not for the additional *mitzvah* of *hiddur mitzvah*.

Thus, the question of how many candles a minor who is lighting because of *chinuch* should light on every night after the first would be contingent on the above-mentioned speculation: If the *hiddur mitzvah* becomes a part of the *mitzvah* itself, then the minor who is being taught to perform the *mitzvah* should do it with *hiddur* and thus add a candle each night.

However if it is not part of the actual *mitzvah*, but rather a separate *halachah* that a *mitzvah* should be performed in a beautiful manner, then the obligation on the father is only to teach his son to perform all the 613 *mitzvot*, including *mitzvot* which are of Rabbinic origin. He is thus not obligated to train him in the separate matter of *hiddur mitzvah*, and the minor should only light one candle each night as training for fulfilling the *mitzvah* to light *Chanukah* candles.

(מחצית השקל ופרי מגדים סי׳ תרע״ו לבוש ופר״ח סי׳ תרע״ב,
שפת אמת עמ״ס שבת, גבורת יצחק סי׳ ח׳)

מָעוֹז צוּר

It is customary in many communities to sing the following hymn after the kindling of the *Chanukah* lights. *Chabad* does not follow this custom.

The hymn consists of six stanzas. The author's name, Mordechai (מרדכי), appears in the acrostic signature in the initial letters of the first five stanzas. The date of its composition seems to have been in the mid-thirteenth century. Whether the last stanza formed part of the original composition or was added later is the subject of some disagreement.

לְךָ נָאֶה לְשַׁבֵּחַ.	מָעוֹז צוּר יְשׁוּעָתִי
וְשָׁם תּוֹדָה נְזַבֵּחַ.	תִּכּוֹן בֵּית תְּפִלָּתִי
מִצָּר הַמְנַבֵּחַ.	לְעֵת תָּכִין מַטְבֵּחַ
חֲנֻכַּת הַמִּזְבֵּחַ:	אָז אֶגְמוֹר בְּשִׁיר מִזְמוֹר
בְּיָגוֹן כֹּחִי כָּלָה.	רָעוֹת שָׂבְעָה נַפְשִׁי
בְּשִׁעְבּוּד מַלְכוּת עֶגְלָה.	חַיַּי מָרְרוּ בְּקוֹשִׁי
הוֹצִיא אֶת הַסְּגֻלָּה.	וּבְיָדוֹ הַגְּדוֹלָה
יָרְדוּ כְּאֶבֶן בִּמְצוּלָה:	חֵיל פַּרְעֹה וְכָל זַרְעוֹ
וְגַם שָׁם לֹא שָׁקַטְתִּי.	דְּבִיר קָדְשׁוֹ הֱבִיאַנִי
כִּי זָרִים עָבַדְתִּי.	וּבָא נוֹגֵשׂ וְהִגְלַנִי
כִּמְעַט שֶׁעָבַרְתִּי.	וְיַיִן רַעַל מָסַכְתִּי
לְקֵץ שִׁבְעִים נוֹשַׁעְתִּי:	קֵץ בָּבֶל. זְרֻבָּבֶל.
אֲגָגִי בֶּן הַמְּדָתָא.	כְּרוֹת קוֹמַת בְּרוֹשׁ בִּקֵּשׁ
וְנַאֲוָתוֹ נִשְׁבָּתָה.	וְנִהְיָתָה לּוֹ לְפַח וּלְמוֹקֵשׁ
וְאוֹיֵב שְׁמוֹ מָחִיתָ.	רֹאשׁ יְמִינִי נִשֵּׂאתָ
עַל הָעֵץ תָּלִיתָ:	רֹב בָּנָיו וְקִנְיָנָיו

I. Prayer for the Re-establishment of the Temple
O mighty stronghold Who is my salvation,
    it is fitting to praise You.
Restore the house of my prayer,
    and there we will bring a thanksgiving offering.
In the time that You will prepare the slaughter
    of the blaspheming oppressor;
Then I will complete a melodious song
    for the dedication of the Altar.

II. The Bondage of Egypt
My soul was sated with troubles
    my strength was consumed with grief.
My life they embittered with hard labor
    in the bondage of the calf-like kingdom.
But through His great hand
    He brought out the precious ones,
The army of Paroah and his offspring
    sank like a stone in the deep.

III. The Babylonian Exile
He brought me to the holy Temple (in Jerusalem),
    Yet even there I had no tranquility.
For an oppressor came and exiled me,
    all because I served alien gods,
and indulged in poisonous wine.
Shortly after my departure,
Babylon came to an end and [our leader] Zerubavel came.
At the end of seventy years I was saved.

IV. Persia and the Purim Miracle
To cut the towering cypress (Mordechai),
    desired the Aggadite (Haman), son of Hamedata.
But his plot trapped and ensnared him,
    and his arrogance was stilled.
The leader of Benjamin You lifted,
    as for the enemy, his name You obliterated.
His many children — his possessions —
    On the gallows You hanged.

יְוָנִים נִקְבְּצוּ עָלַי   אֲזַי בִּימֵי חַשְׁמַנִּים.

וּפָרְצוּ חוֹמוֹת מִגְדָּלַי   וְטִמְּאוּ כָּל הַשְּׁמָנִים.

וּמִנּוֹתַר קַנְקַנִּים   נַעֲשָׂה נֵס לַשּׁוֹשַׁנִּים.

בְּנֵי בִינָה יְמֵי שְׁמוֹנָה   קָבְעוּ שִׁיר וּרְנָנִים:

חֲשׂוֹף זְרוֹעַ קָדְשֶׁךָ   וְקָרֵב קֵץ הַיְשׁוּעָה.

נְקֹם נִקְמַת דַּם עֲבָדֶיךָ   מֵאֻמָּה הָרְשָׁעָה.

כִּי אָרְכָה לָּנוּ הַשָּׁעָה   וְאֵין קֵץ לִימֵי הָרָעָה.

דְּחֵה אַדְמוֹן בְּצֵל צַלְמוֹן   הָקֵם לָנוּ רוֹעִים שִׁבְעָה:

"וּפרצו חומות מגדלי"

"They breached the walls of my towers."

QUESTION: Which walls did they breach?

ANSWER: The *Beit Hamikdash* stood on a mountain which was 1500 cubits square. Around the mountain was a wall. Inside the wall was the *soreig* — a wood fence of lattice work ten handbreadths tall — which stood ten cubits away from the wall of the *Azarah* — Temple Court. The *soreig* served as a sign that non-Jews and Jews defiled by a corpse could not enter any further (see *Keilim* 1:8). The Syrian-Greeks made thirteen breaches in the *soreig* wall. When the Hasmoneans regained control over the *Beit Hamikdash,* they repaired the damage. The Sages also instituted that one prostrate himself thirteen times, once at each of the sites of these breaches as an expression of gratitude to Hashem for delivering the Jews and destroying the Syrian-Greek Empire.

(מדות פ"ב מ"ג)

"וּפרצו חומות מגדלי"

"They breached the walls of my towers."

QUESTION: Why did they breach the *soireg* wall specifically?

V. The Miraculous *Chanukah* Victory
Greeks gathered against me,
    then, in the days of the Hasmoneans.
They breached the walls of my towers,
    and defiled all the oils.
And from the remnant of the flasks
    a miracle was wrought for the roses (the Jews).
Men of insight: Eight days
    established for song and celebration.

VI. Plea for the Final Redemption
Bare Your Holy arm
    and hasten the End for salvation.
Avenge the blood of Your servants from the evil nation.
For the hour has grown long for us,
    and there is no end to the days of evil
Repel the red one (Rome) into the nethermost shadows;
    and establish for us the seven shepherds.

ANSWER: The Syrian-Greeks did not seek the physical annihilation, G-d forbid, of the Jewish people. Rather, they sought a spiritual obliteration, to detach the Jews from tenacious attachment to Hashem and to remove any demarcation that existed between Jew and non-Jew. Hence, once a Jew Hellenized and accepted their philosophy, he was spared persecution. Thus, they objected to this wall that marked the farthest point a non-Jew may go on the Temple Mount and they breached it.

(תוס׳ יום טוב, שם)

"ופרצו חומות מגדלי"

"They breached the walls of my towers."

QUESTION: Why did they make exactly thirteen breaches in the *soireg* wall, not more or less?

ANSWER: In the *Al Hanissim* prayer we say that the goal of the Syrian-Greeks was *"lehashkicham Toratecha"* — "to make the Jewish people to forget Your Torah." The emphasis *"Toratecha"* — "Your Torah" — and not just *"HaTorah"* —

"the Torah" — is because they were not against the Jews studying Torah, but wanted that Torah should be approached as an intellectual study and not as the holy wisdom of Hashem

In our daily morning prayers we quote the teaching of Rabbi Yishmael that Torah is expounded by means of thirteen rules. If Torah would be human intellect, then this would not be applicable. Only because it is Divinely given can Torah be interpreted and studied in all these ways although all the conclusions derived were originally conveyed by the Giver — Hashem, blessed be He. With the thirteen breaches the Syrian-Greeks were alluding to their view that the Torah was not G-d given and could not be studied with the thirteen different approaches.

(עי' בפתחא זעירא לספר נטעי גבריאל על חנוכה)

Alternatively, the number thirteen is also the numerical value of the word *"echad"* (אחד), which signifies oneness and unity. In the *Al Hanissim* prayer we proclaim that Hashem gave over *"rabbim beyad me'attim"* — "many into the *hand* of the few." The success of the Jewish people was due to the unity that prevailed. The Syrian-Greek's message was that they would endeavor to destroy the unity of the Jewish people and thus defeat them. Fortunately, the righteous and pure remained steadfastly united, and the enemy's devious plans failed.

* * *

Due to the audacity shown by the Syrian-Greeks when they damaged Hashem's holy property by making thirteen breaches, Hashem responded with His Thirteen Attributes of Mercy and brought about the salvation of His beloved people — *Klal Yisrael.*

"ופרצו חומות מגדלי וטמאו כל השמנים"

"They breached the walls of my towers and they defiled all the oils."

QUESTION: What is the connection between these two iniquities of the Syrian-Greeks?

ANSWER: The finding of the single sealed flask of oil was a great miracle since the Syrian-Greeks defiled all the oil in the *Beit Hamikdash*. However, a difficulty raised about this is that the *Gemara* (*Pesachim* 18a) says that liquids of the *Beit Hamikdash* are not susceptible to *tumah* — defilement?

An answer to this question is that the *halachah* applies only as long as the sanctity of the *Beit Hamikdash* is in effect; then the wine and oil therein cannot become *tamei*. If, however, it has lost its sanctity, then it no longer protects the liquids against *tumah*. In such an instance, oil within the confines of such a *Beit Hamikdash* is equivalent to oil which was taken outside of the *Beit Hamikdash* and is no longer protected and indeed can become *tamei* (see ibid. 17b).

The *Gemara* (*Avodah Zarah* 52b) says that the Syrian-Greeks defiled the Altar by sacrificing an offering to an idol. Once this occurred, the Rabbis applied the *pasuk* "and lawless people came into [the Sanctuary] and profaned it" (Ezekiel 7:22). That is, through their behavior in the *Beit Hamikdash,* they caused it to be stripped of its sanctity.

Hence, the hymn is stating; since *"upartzu chomot migdalai"* — "they breached the walls of my towers" — i.e. the lawless people entered into it, and profaned it, causing it to lose its sanctity, *"tim'u kol hashemanin"* — they were able to defile all the oils therein.

(שו"ת בית יצחק או"ח סי' כ"ז)

"ומנותר קנקנים נעשה נס לשושנים"

"From the remnant of the flasks a miracle was wrought for the roses."

QUESTION: The miracle of *Chanukah* was with the *pach hashemen* — flask of oil. So instead of *"kankanim"* it should have said *"pachim"*?

ANSWER: In *Pirkei Avot* (4:20) Rabbi Meir says *"Al tistakeil bakankan elah bamah sheyeish bo"* — "Do not look at the vessel rather by what it contains." Which *kankan* was Rabbi Meir advising us not to look at, and what does it contain?

In the Thirteen Attributes of Mercy listed in the Torah
(*Shemot* 34:6, 7), it is written, "Preserver of kindness for two
thousand generations, Forgiver of iniquity, willful
transgression and sin, and *venakeih lo yenakeh* — He absolves
but does not cleanse completely" (see Rashi). How does
"*venakeih lo yenakeh*" fit in to the Attributes of Mercy?

The word "*kankan*" (קנקן) — "vessel" — is composed of
the middle letters of the words "*venakeih yenakeh*" (ונקה ינקה).
Possibly, Rabbi Meir is alluding that when we look at the
words "*venakeih lo yenakeh*" (ונקה לא ינקה) they do not appear to
fit among the Thirteen Attributes of Mercy. However, when
we remove the "נק" from "ונקה", and the "ינק" from "ינקה",
then each word spells half of Hashem's name (יה, ה-ו, ה). Hence,
by not looking at the letters "קנקן," the words "ונקה לא ינקה" fit
very well among the Thirteen Attributes of Mercy.

Thus, Rabbi Meir is offering words of consolation, that no
Jew should despair when reading of His Attributes of Mercy
since also in "*venakeih lo yenakeh*" there is hidden mercy.

The Hymnist's message is that all the miracles Hashem
performed for the Jewish people on *Chanukah* were thanks to
His mercy. He hints it to us in the following way: *U'minotar
kankanim* — from the remnant after you remove the *kankanim*
— (i.e. the four letters which spell the word "*kan*" two times)
from *venakeih yenahek*, you are left with His holy four letter
Name, which connotes mercy. Hence from this remnant
which spells out His attribute of mercy, a miracle was
wrought for the roses, i.e. the Jewish people.

(בני יששכר)

"ומנותר קנקנים נעשה נס לשושנים"

**"From the remnant of the flasks a miracle
was wrought for the roses."**

QUESTION: What remnant is the hymnist referring to?

ANSWER: The *Beit Yosef* questions that *Chanukah* should
be celebrated for only seven days because for the first day oil
was available without any miracles? One of the answers is

that after filling the *Menorah* on the first night, some oil remained in the flask which later miraculously increased so that they had oil for the next night. Thus, there was a miracle also on the first day and this repeated itself every day.

The hymnist is alluding to this explanation and telling us that the miracle of *Chanukah* was that *u'minotar kankanin* — from the remnant oil which remained in the flask a miracle was wrought for the roses.

(נר מצוה)

"נעשה נס לשושנים"
"A miracle was wrought for the roses."

QUESTION: In what way are the Jewish people analogous to a rose?

ANSWER: According to the *Midrash*, "When a rose is among thorns, a north wind goes forth and bends her toward the south and a thorn pricks her, then a south wind goes forth and bends her toward the north and a thorn pricks her; yet, for all that, her core is directed upwards. The same is true with the Jewish people. Although they are oppressed and tortured from all sides by the nations, their hearts are directed towards their Father in Heaven."

(מדרש רבה ויקרא כג:ה)

Once, while the Ramban (Nachmanides) and a priest were taking a stroll together in a garden, the priest said, "You Jews must be a terrible people; otherwise, why do all the nations of the world torture and despise you?" The Ramban took him to a section in the garden where there were beautiful rose bushes in the midst of thorns, and said to him, "Does the fact that these roses are pricked by the thorns and bitten by insects depict the superiority of the thorns and the insects, and the inadequacy of the rose? Of course not; it is merely that the refined and tender rose is incapable of standing up to the strong and vicious thorns. Likewise, their persecuting us is no proof of their superiority and our inadequacy. They are coarse and rough, and we are physically weak and delicate."

(פון אונזער אלטען אוצר)

"ויקרב קץ הישועה"

"And hasten the End for salvation."

QUESTION: Why is the ultimate redemption called *"keitz"*?

ANSWER: At the *"Brit Bein Habetarim"* — "Covenant Between the Parts" — Hashem said to Avraham, "Your offspring shall be aliens in a land not their own, and they will oppress them four hundred years" (*Bereishit* 15:13). The fulfillment of this vision was the Egyptian exile and servitude. Commentaries ask, however: The Jewish people were in Egypt only for a total of 210 years — why did Hashem say 400 years"?

Among the numerous explanations to this question is the following: Whatever Hashem says is definitely true. However, Hashem did not say 400 years in Egypt, rather "in a land not their own." This could have been in Egypt, however, the Jews sunk there to such a spiritual low ebb that had they been there any longer, they would not be worthy to be redeemed. Hence, Hashem was forced to take them out of Egypt prematurely. The remaining 190 years of the prophecy is being fulfilled with our subjugations under the Four Monarchies, Babylon, Media-Persia, Syrian-Greeks and Rome. The word *"keitz"* — "end" — (קץ) has the numerical value of 190, and this end will be heralded with the coming of *Mashiach*.

(עי' הגש"פ ע"פ ילקוט שמעוני ע' 74 בשם בנין אריאל)

"ויקרב קץ הגאולה"

"Hasten the End for salvation."

QUESTION: What is the meaning of *"hasten the end"*?

ANSWER: Regarding the redemption the Prophet says, *"Be'itah achishenah"* — "In its time I will hasten it" (Isaiah 60:22). The phrase "in its time," i.e. at its predetermined time, apparently contradicts the phrase "I will hasten it" which implies that the redemption will come earlier. The *Gemara* (*Sanhedrin* 98a) explains that there is *"be'itah"* — "a preordained time" — for the redemption but Hashem may decide *"achishenah"* — "to hasten" — the redemption before the preordained time. If the Jews are deserving, then, *"Achishenah"* — "I will hasten it." If they are not deserving, then, *"Be'itah"* — "[It will occur] in its time."

Thus, our prayer is that Hashem redeem us hastily and send *Mashiach* instantaneously.

* * *

Incidentally, regarding the coming of *Mashiach* it is commonly accepted that Eliyahu will herald his coming. Nevertheless, the Rambam (*Melachim* 12:2) says that "Among the *chachamim* — wise men — some say that Eliyahu will appear prior to the coming of *Mashiach*. However, man will not know this clearly until it actually happens...and therefore there are disputes about this."

Commentaries explain that the Rambam is not disputing what is commonly accepted about Eliyahu and *Mashiach*, but rather that there are two ways in which the revelation of *Mashiach* may take place and this determines whether Eliyahu will precede or follow the coming of *Mashiach*.

Should we have to wait for the redemption to happen in the preordained time, then it will be heralded by Eliyahu. However, if it is hastened, then all established decorum will be negated and *Mashiach* will arrive unexpectedly and unannounced.

(שו"ת בית יחזקאל מר' צבי יחזקאל ז"ל מיכלזון, כרתי ופלתי יו"ד סוף סי' ק"י)

עַל הַנִּסִּים

וְעַל הַנִּסִּים וְעַל הַפֻּרְקָן וְעַל הַגְּבוּרוֹת וְעַל הַתְּשׁוּעוֹת וְעַל הַנִּפְלָאוֹת שֶׁעָשִׂיתָ לַאֲבוֹתֵינוּ בַּיָּמִים הָהֵם בַּזְּמַן הַזֶּה:

בִּימֵי מַתִּתְיָהוּ בֶּן יוֹחָנָן כֹּהֵן גָּדוֹל, חַשְׁמוֹנָאִי וּבָנָיו, כְּשֶׁעָמְדָה מַלְכוּת יָוָן הָרְשָׁעָה, עַל עַמְּךָ יִשְׂרָאֵל, לְהַשְׁכִּיחָם תּוֹרָתֶךָ וּלְהַעֲבִירָם מֵחֻקֵּי רְצוֹנֶךָ, וְאַתָּה בְּרַחֲמֶיךָ הָרַבִּים עָמַדְתָּ לָהֶם בְּעֵת צָרָתָם. רַבְתָּ אֶת רִיבָם, דַּנְתָּ אֶת דִּינָם, נָקַמְתָּ אֶת נִקְמָתָם. מָסַרְתָּ גִבּוֹרִים בְּיַד חַלָּשִׁים, וְרַבִּים בְּיַד מְעַטִּים, וּטְמֵאִים בְּיַד טְהוֹרִים, וּרְשָׁעִים בְּיַד צַדִּיקִים, וְזֵדִים בְּיַד עוֹסְקֵי תוֹרָתֶךָ. וּלְךָ עָשִׂיתָ שֵׁם גָּדוֹל וְקָדוֹשׁ בְּעוֹלָמֶךָ, וּלְעַמְּךָ יִשְׂרָאֵל עָשִׂיתָ תְּשׁוּעָה גְדוֹלָה וּפֻרְקָן כְּהַיּוֹם הַזֶּה. וְאַחַר כַּךְ בָּאוּ בָנֶיךָ לִדְבִיר בֵּיתֶךָ, וּפִנּוּ אֶת הֵיכָלֶךָ, וְטִהֲרוּ אֶת מִקְדָּשֶׁךָ, וְהִדְלִיקוּ נֵרוֹת בְּחַצְרוֹת קָדְשֶׁךָ, וְקָבְעוּ שְׁמוֹנַת יְמֵי חֲנֻכָּה אֵלּוּ לְהוֹדוֹת וּלְהַלֵּל לְשִׁמְךָ הַגָּדוֹל:

"בימי מתתיהו בן יוחנן כהן גדול"

"In the days of Matityahu,
the son of Yochanan the High Priest."

QUESTION: The *Al Hanissim* recited on *Purim* just says "In the days of Mordechai" without mentioning his father; why on *Chanukah* do we mention that Matityahu was the son of Yochanan the *Kohen Gadol*?

ANSWER: A group of young *kohanim* of the Chashmoneam house went out before *Yom Kippur* to fight the Greeks and waged war on *Yom Kippur*. When Yochanan the *Kohen Gadol* came to the *Beit Hamikdash* to perform the special service of the day, he heard a Heavenly voice emanating from the Holy of Holies, proclaiming: "The young men who went to wage war in Antioch have been victorious" (see *Sotah* 33a).

Al Hanissim

And [we thank You] for the miracles, for the redemption, for the mighty deeds, for the saving acts, and for the wonders which You have wrought for our ancestors in those days, at this time:

In the days of Matityahu, the son of Yochanan the High Priest, the Hasmonean and his sons, when the wicked Hellenic government rose up against Your people Israel to make them forget Your Torah and violate the decrees of Your will. But You, in Your abounding mercies, stood by them in the time of their distress. You waged their battles, defended their rights and avenged the wrong done to them. You delivered the mighty into the hand of the weak, the many into the hand of the few, the impure into the hand of the pure, the wicked into the hand of the righteous, and the wanton sinners into the hand of those who occupy themselves with Your Torah. You made a great and holy name for Yourself in Your world, and effected a great deliverance and redemption for Your people to this very day. Then Your children entered the shrine of Your House, cleansed Your Temple, purified Your Sanctuary, kindled lights in Your holy courtyards, and instituted these eight days of *Chanukah* to give thanks and praise to Your great Name.

Since Yochanan merited to be informed of a victory of the Hasmoneans over the Greeks, his name is mentioned in the prayer of praise to Hashem for the victories.

(בני יששכר מאמר ד' סי' כ"ח)

"בימי מתתיהו בן יוחנן"

"In the days of Matityahu, the son of Yochanan"

QUESTION: What impact did Yochanan have on our way of celebrating the miracle of *Chanukah?*

ANSWER: The *Gemara* (*Sotah* 48a) says that "until the days of Yochanan the *Kohen Gadol,* the hammer [of the blacksmith] would bang in Jerusalem [on *Chol Hamo'eid* — the intermediate days of *Pesach* and *Sukkot*] and he forbade it."

While many forms of work are forbidden on *Chol Hamo'eid,* tasks necessary to prevent irretrievable loss are permitted. The blacksmiths were thus permitted to perform their work on *Chol Hamo'eid* in order to prevent an irretrievable loss (see *Mo'eid Kattan* 11a). Nevertheless, Yochanan the *Kohen Gadol* decreed that they should not perform this work because the loud noise of the hammers banging on the anvil was heard a far distance away. He was concerned that some would not know that the noise was from the blacksmiths who were performing their work, which is permitted, and that they would mistakenly assume that all work is permitted. Therefore, he forbade the banging of the hammer on *Chol Hamo'eid.*

With the prohibition of causing the loud noises he caused the people to refrain from work and assured the sanctity of *Chol Hamo'eid.* Therefore, as a reward, he merited that through his son a *Yom Tov* was added for the Jewish people in which *pirsumei nisa* — publicizing of the miracle — is a an essential prerequisite for proper observance.

*   *   *

Perhaps this may also be a reason for the opinion that everyone (not only women) should refrain from doing work while the candles which publicize the miracle are lit.

(בני יששכר מאמר ד' סי' כ"א, בענין איסור מלאכה כשהנרות דולקות עי' ב"ח סי' עת"ר בשם מהרי"ל
"שקבלה בידינו שאין לאדם לעשות מלאכה בשעה שהנרות דולקים בחנוכה" ועי' בדרכי יוסף)

"לְהַשְׁכִּיחָם תּוֹרָתֶיךָ"

"To make them forget Your Torah."

QUESTION: The Syrian-Greeks endeavored to make the Jews cease studying Torah and instead study Greek

Mythology and other secular subjects. Hence, instead of *"Lehashkicham Toratecha"* — "To make them forget Your Torah" — it should have said *"Levatlam milumud Toratecha"* — "To void them from the study of Your Torah"?

ANSWER: According to the *Midrash* (*Bereishit Rabbah* 2:4), when the Torah (*Bereishit* 1:2) says "'and there was darkness [upon the face of the deep]' — darkness symbolizes Greece, which darkened the eyes of Israel with its decrees."

Torah is the light by which the Jewish people exist. Without Torah we are in the darkness. The word *"lehaskicham"* includes the letters of the word *"choshech"* (חשך) — "darkness." With this term the authors of the prayer wanted to emphasize the wickedness of the Syrian-Greeks. The reason they wanted *lehashkicham* — to make the Jews forget Hashem's Torah — was that through this we would lose our guiding light and live in spiritual darkness.

(בני יששכר)

"נקמת נקמתם"

"You avenged the wrong done to them."

QUESTION: *"Nekamah"* literally means "revenge," in which one requites a wrong done to him by another, by performing a similar act. Rashi (*Vayikra* 19:18) gives the following example: "One man said to another "Lend me your sickle and the second said to him, 'No.' The next day the second said to the first, 'Lend me your hatchet.' The first one replied, 'I am not lending it to you just as you did not lend to me.' This is taking revenge." What revenge did Hashem take for the Jews?

ANSWER: According to the *Midrash* (see *Aruch Hashulchan* 670:5, *Seder Hadorot*, p. 145) the Syrian-Greeks prevented the Jews from celebrating the eight days of *Sukkot* and bringing the many required festival offerings in the *Beit Hamikdash*. As a *nekamah* — revenge — Hashem gave the Jews a new eight day festival — *Chanukah*.

Alternatively, the Syrian-Greeks demanded that the Jews write on the horn of the ox that they denied their belief and share in the G-d of Israel. Their intent was that they should publicize their *kefirah* — heresy. As a *nekamah* — revenge, Hashem gave us a *mitzvah* of kindling the *Chanukah Menorah* and it must be done with *pisumei nisa* — publicizing the miracle. Thus, everyone will know what Hashem did for us thanks to our allegiance and dedication to Him.

(הרב דוב צבי שי' קרלנשטיין, קונטרס בעניני חנוכה)

"מסרת גבורים ביד חלשים ורבים ביד מעטים וטמאים ביד טהורים
ורשעים ביד צדיקים וזדים ביד עוסקי תורתך"

"You delivered the mighty into the hand of the weak, the many into the hand of the few, the impure into the hand of the pure, the wicked into the hand of the righteous, and the wanton sinners into the hand of those who occupy themselves with your Torah."

QUESTION: For the weak and few to be able to conquer the strong and many is a miracle, but what miracle is it that impure were conquered by the pure or that the righteous conquered the wicked?

ANSWER: According to the historians, in addition to those who succumbed to the Greek-Syrians' decrees against Torah and *mitzvot* due to the extreme pressure, there were also many Jews who were known as *"Mityavnim"* — "Hellenized Jews." These people agreed with the Greek philosophy and were antagonistic toward the minority of Jews who remained steadfast and faithful to Hashem.

The weak and few dedicated Jews not only fought the *Yevanim* — the Greeks — but also the *Mityavnim* — the Jews who accepted Hellenistic philosophy. They are the *"temei'im"* — "impure" — *"resha'im"* — "wicked" — and *"zeidim"* — "wanton sinners" — referred to in this prayer.

Thus, the miracle that occurred in regard to them was twofold:

1) They were conquered though they were a majority and an internal enemy is worse that an external one.

2) Hashem gave them "over" (מסרת) into the hands of their Torah committed brothers and they repented and accepted the ways of the pure, the righteous, and those engaged in Torah study.

A compelling reason for this explanation is that otherwise the descriptions of impure, wicked, and wanton sinners would be difficult to comprehend as referring to the Syrian-Greeks. The concept of *tumah* and *taharah* does not apply to non-Jews. In matters of *tumah* — impurity — just as a live animal does not become *tamei,* so don't non-Jews (see Rambam, *Tumat Meit,* 1:13).

The term *"tzaddik"* and *"rasha"* — *"righteous"* and *"wicked"* — are reserved specifically for Jews contingent on their observance of Torah and *mitzvot* or the lack of it and their reward or punishment for Torah compliance or violation (see *Likkutei Sichos,* Vol. 5, p. 159).

The term *"oiseik baTorah"* — engaged in Torah study — does not apply to non-Jews. In fact, the *Gemara (Sanhedrin* 59a) says that a gentile who engages in Torah study is liable death punishment. If so, the term *"zeidim"* — "wanton sinners" — which is a description of those opposing the Torah studiers, cannot be a categorization of the non-Jews.

The *mityavnim,* who were Jews, were at that time unfortunately *"tamei'im"* — "impure" — *"resha'im"* — "wicked" — and *"zeidim"* — "wanton sinners," who miraculously were *"mosarta"* — "given over" — by Hashem into the control of the pure and righteous Jews who engaged in Torah study.

(לקוטי שיחות ח"ל ע' 209)

"ואחר כך באו בניך לדביר ביתך ופינו את היכלך וטהרו את מקדשך"

"After that Your children entered the shrine of Your House, cleansed Your Temple, purified Your Sanctuary."

QUESTION: Why did the Rabbis who authored this prayer include the two words *"v'achar kach,"* — "and after that" — which seem to be superfluous?

ANSWER: For a moment let us picture the situation: We find a mighty army ready to do battle with the people of Israel, who are absolutely unprepared militarily. They possess neither the numbers nor the arms to prevail against the enemy. We can imagine what took place when a man left his home to go to the battlefront, knowing his side was outnumbered and unprepared to win the war. His family, of course, is broken-hearted. His wife, children, and in many cases brothers and sisters bid farewell to the young man with trepidation, not knowing whether or not they would see him alive again.

Finally the battle takes place and a miracle occurs. The tide is turned. Instead of the many being victorious over the few, the mighty over the weak, it is the other way around. Matityahu's sons and the Hasmonean armies are victorious and win the war. Now, it stands to reason that the first reaction from the soldiers should be to immediately rush back home and tell their families that they are alive, safe and sound.

However, it wasn't so. After winning the war, these men first went to the Holy Temple to rid it of impurities, re-establish its sanctity and try to bring back the G-dly light of the *Menorah*. Therefore, our Rabbis tell us *"v'achar kach"* — "and after that" — i.e. after it was over — they did not run home to their families and bring them the good tidings. No, they first went to the Holy Temple, for they knew that winning a physical battle wasn't everything. They felt that until the house of Hashem was put in order, their victory was not complete. Our Rabbis wanted to impress upon us that these men who went out to battle realized that the greatest accomplishment would be to put the House of Hashem back in order. And this was the first obligation they proceeded to fulfill immediately after claiming victory.

(הרב יעקב יהודה ז"ל העכט)

Alternatively, by these actions they demonstrated that their interest in the battle was not military victory, nor political power, but undisturbed service of Hashem and study of His Torah. Therefore the first thing they did after their victory was coming to the *Beit Hamikdash*.

(חפץ חיים)

"והדליקו נרות בחצרות קדשך"
"And they kindled lights in Your holy courtyards."

QUESTION: The kindling of the *Menorah* took place in the *Beit Hamikdash* itself. Why did the Hasmoneans kindle it in the courtyard?

ANSWER: When the Hasmoneans entered the *Beit Hamikdash*, they found it defiled and in ruins. Thus, they were unable to kindle the *Menorah* while it stood in its regular place. In the interim, while they were cleaning the mess and renovating, the *Menorah* was kindled in the courtyard. This is permissible according to *halachah* (see Rambam, *Hilchot Biat Hamikdash* 9:7).

Through kindling the *Menorah* in the courtyard, everyone was able to witness the eight-day miracle, which would not have been the case had it been lit inside. Then, only the *Kohanim* would have seen it.

With this explanation, we can answer the popular question: Why *Chanukah* is celebrated for eight-days rather than seven, though sufficient oil was found for the first night.

The oil found would have lasted through the night only if the *Menorah* would have been kindled *inside*. However, *Chanukah* takes place during the winter, and due to weather conditions, the oil would normally not have been sufficient to last through the night when the *Menorah* was kindled outside in the courtyard.

(חתם סופר)

The Lubavitcher Rebbe questions: According to this, grammatically it should be in singular: ***"bechatzer kadeshecha"*** — "in Your holy courtyard" — in lieu of the plural, *"bechatzrot kadeshecha"* — "in Your holy courtyards." Thus, he asserts that the *Menorah* was indeed kindled *inside* the *Beit Hamikdash*. However, as an additional expression of joy and happiness, all the courtyards in the outskirts of the *Beit Hamikdash* were also illuminated with an abundance of light.

(לקוטי שיחות חכ"ה ע' 238, וכ' האבודרהם "בחצרות קדשיך
ע"ש [ישעי' ס"ב ט'] בחצרות קדשי" ושם מדובר ע"ד העיר ירושלים)

פרסומי ניסא

Publicizing the Miracle

PIRSUMEI NISA
DECLARE ON THE HORN OF AN OX
KINGDOM OF THE HASMONEANS
CHANUKAH — SUKKOT
THE *DUDAIM* EMIT A FRAGRANCE...

פרסומי ניסא
Publicizing the Miracle

"נר חנוכה מצוה להניחה על פתח ביתו מבחוץ"

"The requirement is to place the *Chanukah* light by the doorway of one's house, from the outside." (*Shabbat* 21b)

QUESTION: Rashi writes that this is because of *pirsumei nisa* — to publicize the miracle. Why on *Chanukah* is *pirsumei nisa* emphasized as a prerequisite for proper fulfillment of the *mitzvah*?

ANSWER: The Syrian-Greeks endeavored to detach the Jews from Torah study. However, they did not suffice with this evil plan, but also demanded that the Jews write on the horn of the ox that they were denouncing their share in the G-d of Israel (*Midrash Rabbah, Bereishit* 2:4).

They made the strange request that the Jewish people use the horn of the ox because in those days it was customary to travel on wagons and chariots which were driven by oxen. The oxen would span the roads and go from place to place, and the horn is the most prominent and visible part of the ox. Therefore, they demanded that their denial in Hashem be written on the ox's horn so that it would receive the widest publicity possible.

To counteract this, our Sages required that when we fulfill the *mitzvah* of lighting the *Menorah*, which commemorates the miracle Hashem did because of our allegiance to Him, it is to be done so as to attract the most public attention possible.

(עי' יפה תואר על מד"ר בראשית ב:ד)

"עד דכליא ריגלא דתרמודאי"

"Until the Tarmodians have vanished from the market." (Shabbat 21b)

QUESTION: The *Chanukah Menorah* is kindled on the outside of one's home because of *Pirsumei Nisa* — the requirement to publicize the miracle. This same concept is also found in regard to drinking four cups of wine on *Pesach* (*Maggid Mishnah, Chanukah* 4:12), and also a reason for folding the *Megillah* to resemble a written letter when it is read on *Purim* (Rambam, *Megillah* 2:12).

Why in those instances is the miracle publicized on the inside — among our Jewish brethren — while on *Chanukah* it is publicized to the non-Jewish world?

ANSWER: Whenever a Jew is thankful about his physical survival, he does not have to communicate it to non-Jews, since physical self-survival is a common instinct among all humans and animals, and it is understood that Jews will fight for their physical survival. This type of miracle does not require publicizing among non-Jews. Thus, *Purim* and *Pesach*, which commemorate our rescue for physical annihilation and slavery, need not be shared with non-Jews since they are well cognizant that Jews like any other human beings will fight ferociously for their physical survival.

On *Chanukah*, however, the Jews' spiritual survival and *not* their physical survival was at stake. The message which we wish to convey to non-Jews is that Jews are willing and able to fight for their spiritual survival as well as their physical well-being, and that the Jews returned from the brink of total assimilation and adopted the *Torah,* and reestablished their unique relationship with G-d.

The message of *Chanukah* is more of a sensation to non-Jews than is the message of *Purim* and *Pesach*, and thus, the *pirsumei nissa* conveyed by the *Chanukah* lights is directed at non-Jews as well.

(הרב יוסף דוב הלוי ז"ל סאלאווייטשיק, מבאסטאן)

"צריך ליזהר מאד בהדלקת נרות חנוכה ואפילו עני המתפרנס
מן הצדקה שואל או מוכר כסותו ולוקח שמן להדליק"

**"One must be very careful in the lighting
of *Chanukah* candles, even a poor person who
is supported by charity must borrow or
sell his garment and purchase oil to kindle."**
(*Orach Chaim* 671:1)

QUESTION: A person is required to spend all his
resources only to avoid violating a negative command of the
Torah, but not for the fulfillment of a positive command (see
Orach Chaim 656). So why for the *Chanukah* kindling is an
indigent person required to borrow money in order to fulfill
the *mitzvah*?

ANSWER: The *Gemara* (*Berachot* 6a) says that if a person
contemplated fulfilling a *mitzvah* and was unavoidably
prevented from performing it, Scripture credits him as if he
had fulfilled it. This applies to all *mitzvot* that are done for
Hashem. However, since the purpose of kindling *Chanukah*
lights is *pirsumei nisa* — publicizing the miracle of *Chanukah* —
one who was unable to perform the *mitzvah* due to reasons
beyond his control (poverty) cannot be considered as having
fulfilled the *mitzvah* when the miracle was not actually
publicized in any way by him.

(אבני נזר או"ח ח"ב סי' תק"א)

כתבו על קרן השור
Declare on the Horn of an Ox

"כתבו לכם על קרן השור שאין לכם חלק באלקי ישראל"

"Write on the horn of an ox that you
have no share in the G-d of Israel."
(Jerusalem Talmud, *Chagigah* 2:2)

QUESTION: The *Midrash Rabbah* (*Bereishit* 2:4) comments that the passage "there was darkness on the face of the abyss" (1:2) refers to the Greek monarchs, who darkened the eyes of the Jewish people with their harsh and cruel decrees. They proclaimed that the Jews should write on the horn of an ox that they had no share in the G-d of Israel.

What did the Syrian-Greeks seek to accomplish when the specified that it be written on the *horn* [of the ox]?

ANSWER: The *Gemara* (*Megillah* 14a) says, "David and Solomon, who when installed as king, were anointed with oil spilled on their head from a *keren* — horn — their reign was prolonged. [The horn of an animal is very durable and therefore represents a prolonged reign — *Maharsha*]

The word *"keren"* (קרן) has the numerical value of 350 as do the words *"yimloch le'olam va'ed"* (ימלך לעלם ועד) — "he will reign forever and ever." This alludes that the kingdom of David is forever. Though the Babylonian king Nevuchadnetzar exiled the Jewish people and the reign of the House of David was interrupted, this condition is only temporary, and ultimately kingship will return in the days of King *Mashiach*, the descendant of David, who will rule over the entire world.

It is incumbent upon Jews to anticipate and pray for the speedy coming of *Mashiach*. Thrice daily we recite the prayer "The offspring of Your servant David, (revelation of *Mashiach*) may You speedily cause to flourish." With the edict that the Jews write on the *horn* [of the ox] renouncing their share in the G-d of Israel, the Syrian-Greeks were demanding that they deny that Hashem will speedily send *Mashiach*, the descendant of King David who was anointed with a horn.

(בני יששכר)

"כתבו לכם על קרן השור שאין לכם חלק באלקי ישראל"

"Write on the horn of an ox that you have no share in the G-d of Israel."
(Jerusalem Talmud, *Chagigah* 2:2)

QUESTION: Why did the Syrian-Greeks specify that this declaration be made on the horn of an ox?

ANSWER: The *Midrash* says that the Greeks wanted the Jews to abolish their calendar where every month is based on the *Beit Din* sanctifying the new moon. They also sought to stop the Jews from observing the laws of *Milah* — circumcision — and *Shabbat*. The Greeks wanted the Jewish people to assimilate and be like all the nations of the world. Therefore, they selected these three *mitzvot* in particular because they demonstrate the distinction between the Jewish people and the secular world.

The secular calendar follows the solar cycle while the Jewish calendar is based on the lunar system. This is in fact, the very first commandment given to the Jewish people as a whole immediately prior to their leaving Egypt (see *Shemot* 12:1).

Shabbat is the Divinely mandated day of rest for the Jewish people while the secular world designates Sunday as their day of rest. In fact, according to *halachah* it is forbidden for a gentile to observe *Shabbat* and the *Gemara* (*Sanhedrin* 58b) says that an idolater who ceased working for the entire day of *Shabbat* is liable to death, for it is stated (*Bereishit* 8:22): "Day and night they shall not cease," and if a Noahide transgresses any prohibition that Scripture warns him against, he is liable to death (see also Rambam, *Melachim* 10:9).

Circumcision is a commandment given to Avraham, the first Jew, for him and his offspring for posterity (*Bereishit* 17:9-13). It is a sign of the covenant between Jews and Hashem, and it stamps its bearer as His servant. Since the circumcision ritual is practiced by Jews, it is considered one of the most widely accepted distinctions between Jew and non-Jew.

The *Gemara* (*Bava Kamma* 2b) says that three primary damages were stated in the Torah in regard to an ox. They are *keren* — the horn — i.e. damage done through goring, *shein* — the tooth — i.e. damage done through eating, and *regel* — the foot — i.e. damage done through trampling on things. When an ox causes damage with its tooth — eating — or with the foot — tramping — the owner must pay in full. However, when the ox causes damage with the horn — goring — it depends whether this is the first time or the third time. During the first and second time the ox is considered a *tam* — innocent — i.e. not confirmed as a habitual inflictor of damage, and thus the owner pays only for one half of the damage. Afterwards, the ox is considered a *mu'ad* — warned — and it has been legally confirmed to be a habitual inflictor of damage through *keren*, and the owner is liable for the entire damage.

Now regarding damage done by eating or trampling, there is no difference if the ox belonged to a Jew or to a non-Jew or whether the property damaged belonged to a Jew or non-Jew. In all circumstances the owner must fully compensate the one damaged. However, in regard to *keren* — goring — the *Gemara* (*Bava Kamma* 37b) says "If the ox of a Jew gored the ox of a Canaanite (non-Jew), the Jew is exempt. But if the ox of a Canaanite gored the ox of a Jew, whether the ox that gored was a *tam* or a *mu'ad*, the Canaanite pays full damages."

Since the goal of the Syrian-Greeks was to remove any custom which distinguishes the Jew from the non-Jew, they demanded that the Jew write on the horn of the ox that they were renouncing their association with Hashem. They would

thus cease to distinguish between Jew and non-Jew in the
case of an ox, which causes damage with its horn.

(בני יששכר – מגלה עמוקות פ׳ מקץ)

"כתבו לכם על קרן השור שאין לכם חלק באלקי ישראל"

**"Write on the horn of an ox that you
have no share in the G-d of Israel."
(Jerusalem Talmud, *Chagigah* 2:2)**

QUESTION: What did the Syrian-Greeks reveal about
themselves by insisting that the Jews' declaration be made
"on the *horn* of the ox?"

ANSWER: The *Gemara* (*Bava Kamma* 2b) explains that an
ox can do damage in one of three ways: with its teeth, feet, or
horns.

The *Gemara* further explains that when an ox gores with
its horns, it does so with the intent to cause damage (כוונתו
להזיק) and derives no personal pleasure from the act (אין הנאה
להזיקו).

The *Midrash* allegorically is describing the psychology and
nature of the Hellenistic regime. They made vicious decrees
against the Jewish people to deter them from studying, Torah
and observing *mitzvot*. Like the ox that gores with its horn
and achieves no personal pleasure, they too, had nothing to
gain. Their sadistic intent was solely to inflict suffering upon
defenseless Jews.

(פון אונזער אלטען אוצר)

מלכות חשמונאי
Kingdom of the Hasmoneans

"וכשגברה מלכות בית חשמונאי ונצחום"

"When the royal Hasmonean house overpowered them and vanquished them." (Shabbat 21b)

QUESTION: The Rambam (*Chanukah* 3:1) writes, "The sons of Chashmonai overpowered and killed them and rescued the Jews from their hands. And they elected a king from among the *Kohanim,* and the kingdom returned to Israel for more than 200 years, until the second destruction."

King David said (Psalms 132:11-12) "Hashem has sworn to David, a truth from which He will never retreat: 'From the fruit of your issue I will place upon your throne ... forever and ever, shall [they] sit upon your throne.'" If so, did the Hasmoneans who were *Kohanim* from the tribe of Levi (and not King David's tribe — Yehudah) act correctly when they seized the Kingdom in Israel?

ANSWER: The Ramban in *Bereishit* (49:10) makes a relevant comment on the *pasuk* "The rod shall not depart from Yehudah nor a lawgiver from between his feet until Shiloh (*Mashiach*) arrives and his will be an assemblage of nations." He explains:

> The kings from other tribes, who ruled over Israel after David, went against the wish of their father Yaakov by diverting the inheritance of Yehudah to another tribe. Now they relied on the word of Achiyah the Shilonite, the prophet who anointed Jeroboam, who said, "And I will afflict the seed of David for this, but not forever." But when [the ten tribes of] Israel continued to crown kings one after another from the rest of the tribes, and they did not revert to the kingdom of Yehudah, they transgressed the testament of their ancestor. Therefore, they were accordingly

punished, just as Hosea said, *"They have set up kings, but not from Me."*

This was also the reason for the punishment of the Hasmoneans, who reigned during the Second Temple. They were *Tzaddikim* of the Most High, without whom the learning of Torah and the observance of Commandments would have been forgotten in Israel, and despite this, they suffered such great punishment. The four sons of the old Hasmonean Matityahu: Yehudah the Maccabee, Elazar, Yonathan and Shimon, righteous men who ruled one after another, in spite of all their prowess and success, fell by the sword of their enemies. And ultimately the punishment reached the stage as declared in the *Gemara* (*Bava Batra* 3b), "He who says, 'I come from the house of the Hasmoneans,' is a slave," as they were all destroyed on account of this sin. All the children of the righteous Matityahu the Hasmonean were deposed for this only: they ruled even though they were not of the seed of Yehudah and of the house of David, and thus they completely removed "the scepter" and "the lawgiver" from Yehudah. And their punishment was measure for measure, as the Holy One, blessed be He, caused their slaves (King Herod) to rule over them, and it is they who destroyed them" (Ramban, Chavel Translation, Shilo, 1971).

* * *

A way to justify the action of the Hasmoneans is the following: The *Gemara* (*Sanhedrin* 5a) says that in Babylonia the Jewish people had a *"Reish Galuta"* — "a scepter" — and in *Eretz Yisrael* the leader of the Jews was the *Nasi*. The difference between them was that the "scepter" had more sovereignty and authority than the *Nasi*. Therefore, the authority of the *Reish Galuta* in Babylon also extended to the

Jewish community in *Eretz Yisrael* while the authority of the *Nasi* did not extend to the community in Babylon.

Tosafot writes that the *Reish Galuta's* authority extends to *Eretz Yisrael* because he descended from the male line of the Davidic House, whereas the *Nasi* descended from the female line.

Hence, we see from here that even when there is only maternal lineage to the house of King David, appointment to leadership is not in violation of the instruction of the patriarch Yaakov that "The rod shall not depart from Yehudah nor a lawgiver from between his feet."

All *Kohanim* are descendants of Aaron, the *Kohen Gadol,* and are members of the tribe of Levi. However, Aaron was married to Elisheva bat Aminadav, who was the sister of Nachshon ben Aminadav (*Shemot* 6:23) the *Nasi* of the tribe of Yehudah.

Consequently, all *Kohanim* have paternal lineage to the tribe of Levi, and they also have lineage to the tribe of Yehudah through their ancestor Elisheva. Therefore, the righteous Hasmoneans permitted themselves to assume a position of royalty.

(יערות דבש ח״ב דף פ׳, דפוס ווין תקע״ח)

"וכשגברה מלכות בית חשמונאי ונצחום
בדקו ולא מצאו אלא פך אחד של שמן"

"When the royal Hasmonean house overpowered them and vanquished them, they searched and found only one flask of oil." (*Shabbat* 21b)

QUESTION: What indication did the Hasmoneans have that it was proper for them to assume *Malchut* — royalty?

ANSWER: The *Gemara* (*Megillah* 14a) says "David and Shlomo, when installed as king, were anointed with a *keren* — horn — of oil [the oil was poured on their head from a horn] — their reign was prolonged. However, Saul and Yehu, when installed as king, were anointed with a *pach* — flask — of oil [the oil was poured on their head from a flask] — their reign was not prolonged." The *Maharsha* explains that a flask symbolized a shortened reign since it is usually made of earthenware, which breaks easily when dropped. The horn of an animal, however, is much more durable, and therefore represents a prolonged reign.

The word *"keren"* (קרן) — horn has the numerical value of 350. This is the same numerical value as the words *"yimloch le'olam va'ed"* (ימלך לעלם ועד) — "to reign forever" — a reference to a long lasting reign. The word *"pach"* (פך) — "flask" merely has the numerical value of 100 as does the word *"yimloch"* ימלך — "to reign" — something temporary and not long lasting.

King David was anointed with a horn because his kingdom will be long lasting, and it will ultimately be continued through his descendant King *Mashiach*.

When the Hasmoneans entered the Sanctuary and found a *pach* — flask — of oil they understood this as Heavenly sign that *yimloch* — they should temporarily assume royalty — but it would not be everlasting, for ultimately the kingdom will be returned to the descendants of David.

* * *

Together with the finding of the flask, all witnessed the miracle of the candles of the *Menorah*. The word *"pach"* — "flask" (פך) — together with the word *"neir"* — "candle" (נר) — adds up to 350, the same numerical value as the word *"keren"* — horn. This was understood as a hint that while the Jews would then enjoy a period of royalty, the real glory will be when *Mashiach* the descendant of David, who was anointed with the *keren* — horn — will appear.

(בני יששכר מאמרי חדשי כסלו טבת מאמר ג')

* * *

Incidentally, the Hasmoneans, ascent to kingship was prophesied by King David when he said in Psalms (132:9-10) *"Kohanecha yilbeshu tzedek"* — "Your *Kohanim* will be clothed in righteousness" — i.e. at the time of the miracle of *Chanukah* your priests will temporarily be garbed in royalty — *vachasidecha yeraneinu* — and your devout ones will sing joyously. (*Chanukah* was established as festival days with respect to recital of *Hallel ve'hoda'ah* — praise and thanksgiving — *Shabbat* 21b).

David continues, *"Ba'avur David avdecha al tasheiv p'nei meshichecha"* — "For the sake of David, Your servant, turn not away the face of Your anointed." David prayed that the Jews shouldn't, G-d forbid, suffice with the glory of the Hasmonean kingdom thinking that it is the ultimate achievement. Rather, they should anticipate and merit speedily the revelation of *Mashiach,* the descendant of King David.

(בני יששכר, שם)

חנוכה – סוכות
Chanukah — Sukkot

"חד אמר טעמא דבית שמאי כנגד פרי החג וטעמא דבית הלל
דמעלין בקדש ואין מורידין"

**"One *Amora* said that *Beit Shammai's* reason for
requiring a continual decrease from eight lights
to one corresponds to the bull sacrifices of
Sukkot, and *Beit Hillel's* reason for requiring a
continual increase from one to eight is that in
sacred matters we increase and do not
decrease." (*Shabbat* 21b)**

QUESTION: The rule of *"ma'alin bekodesh"* — [in sacred
matters] we increase" — is mentioned many times in *Gemara*
and is a widely accepted rule. Why does *Beit Shammai*
disregard it and on the contrary, in the case of *Chanukah* he
bases his decision on the progressive diminution of the
Sukkot sacrifices.

ANSWER: According to the *Midrash* the Syrian-Greeks
issued decrees against the observance of the *Sukkot* festival.
They prevented the Jews from bringing the festival sacrifices
and also caused them to endure hardship in order to observe
Sukkot.

Beit Shammai indeed agrees with the popular rule that in
sacred matters we elevate. However, in the instance of
Chanukah they emphasize that since prior to *Chanukah* the
Jews struggled with the *mitzvah* of *Sukkot* and now that they
have been victorious, there will no longer be any deterrent to
observe *Sukkot* in the future. Therefore, they hold that it is
only proper that some law of *Sukkot* be applied to the ways
the *Chanukah* victory is commemorated. Hence, *Beit Shammai*
opine that the *Chanukah* lights should be kindled in a
decreasing number, similar to *Sukkot* sacrifices, which the
Syrian-Greeks forbade to be offered.

(עי' ערוך השלחן סי' עת"ר וסדר הדורות ג"א תרכ"ב)

"וַיַּחְגּוּ חַג לַה׳ שְׁמוֹנַת יָמִים כִּימֵי חַג הַסֻּכּוֹת"

"They celebrated a festival to Hashem for eight days, just as the days of the *Sukkot* festival." (*Sefer Hasmonean II*, 10:9)

QUESTION: What do *Sukkot* and *Chanukah* have in common?

ANSWER: According to a *Midrash* the Greeks issued a decree forbidding the Jews to observe the *Sukkot* festival, and they were unable to bring the sacrificial offerings of *Sukkot* in the *Beit Hamikdash*. Hence, Hashem said, "You wanted to abolish the eight days of *Sukkot;* I will therefore give them an additional festive period of eight days — *Chanukah.*"

(מדרש חנוכה ח״א קל״ד, א. סדר הדורות ג״א תרכ״ב, וערוך השלחן עת״ר סעי׳ ה)

Alternatively, in *Chumash Vayikra*, there is a listing of all the festivals of the year, concluding with *Sukkot*. This is followed immediately by the *Parshah* in which Hashem says to Moshe, "Command the Children of Israel that they take to you pure olive oil, to kindle a lamp continually," (23:1-44, 24:14). The juxtaposition of *Sukkot* to olive oil is an indication that on the eighth day of *Chanukah* we recite the entire *Hallel*, just as it is said in its entirety all the eight days of *Sukkot*.

(בעל הטורים ויקרא כ״ד, ב)

*   *   *

Alternatively, the *Beit Yosef* (*Tur, Orach Chaim* 417) writes in the name of his brother Rabbi Yehudah that the three festivals *Pesach*, *Shavuot*, and *Sukkot* correspond to the patriarchs Avraham, Yitzchak, and Yaakov.

When the angels visited Avraham, he told Sarah, "Hurry! Three *se'ahs* of meal, fine flour! Knead it and make cakes!" (*Bereishit* 18:6). The visit took place on *Pesach* (see Rashi, ibid. 18:10), and the cakes she baked were actually *matzot*. Since it was *Pesach*, he wanted her to prepare the dough herself to guard against leavening (*Alshich*). *Shavuot* commemorates the giving of the Torah and corresponds to Yitzchak because it was heralded by the blast of the *shofar,* which came from the ram which was offered in his stead (*Pirkei D'Rebbe Eliezer,* 31). *Sukkot* is for Yaakov, as the *pasuk* says, "Yaakov journeyed to Sukkot and built himself a house, and for his livestock he made shelters; he therefore called the name of the place 'Sukkot'" (ibid. 33:17).

The name "Yaakov" (יעקב) has the numerical value of one hundred and eighty-two. Since *Sukkot* is in his honor, one hundred and eighty-two sacrifices were offered during the festival.

The three patriarchs were prototypes of the three things (Torah, service [of G-d], and deeds of kindness) upon which the world stands. Avraham was the prototype of *Gemilut Chassadim,* Yitzchak represents *Avodah* — sacrifice and prayer, and Yaakov, who is described in the Torah as "A wholesome man, abiding in the tents [the *yeshivot* of Shem and Eiver (*Bereishit,* 25:22, Rashi)]," is the prototype of Torah.

The Greeks endeavored to detach the Jews from Torah study, which is compared to light, and have them pursue secular knowledge. *Chanukah,* which is connected with light, is thus the holiday in which we celebrate our renewed opportunity to engage in Torah study. So *Sukkot,* which is the festival associated with Yaakov (the prototype of Torah), is most compatible with *Chanukah,* the festival which commemorates our salvation from those who wanted to make us forget Torah.

(קונטרס בעניני חנוכה סי׳ ו׳)

"ויעקב נסע סכתה ויבן לו בית"

"Yaakov journeyed to Sukkot and built for himself a house." (*Bereishit* 33:17)

QUESTION: The word *"lo"* — "for himself" — seems superfluous; it could have just said *"Vayiven bayit"* — "He built a house"?

ANSWER: Here is a *remez* — hint — that Yaakov celebrated *Sukkot* and *Chanukah.* According to the *Zohar*

Vayikra 100b the first point of the *pasuk*, "Yaakov journeyed to Sukkot," is a hint that Yaakov observed *Sukkot*, the festival that corresponds to him (see above).

The second part of the *pasuk*, "He built for himself a house," can be explained as a hint to *Chanukah*. According to the *Gemara* (*Shabbat* 21b) the proper way to fulfill the *mitzvah* of kindling *Chanukah* candles is to place them "*al petach beito mibachutz*" — "by the entrance of one's house from the outside." During the eight days of *Chanukah* we kindle a total of 36 candles (without the *shmashim*). The numerical value of the word "*lo*" (לו) — "for himself" — is 36.

Thus, the Torah tells us not only did Yaakov journey to Sukkot, a hint that he observed *Sukkot*, but he built *lo bayit* — a house where he could kindle 36 candles at the entrance for the eight days of *Chanukah*.

(שפת אמת)

"חנוכה – סוכות"
"Chanukah — Sukkot"

QUESTION: Where in the prophets do we find a connection between *Chanukah* and *Sukkot*?

ANSWER: A connection between *Chanukah* and *Sukkot* is found among is prophesies of Haggai. He was one of the last prophets and one of the *Anshei Keneset HaGedolah* — The Men of the Great Assembly. He lived during the reign of King Darius of Persia, who according to the *Midrash* was the son of Achashveirosh and Esther, and he sanctioned and encouraged the construction of the second *Beit Hamikdash* which had begun in the days of Cyrus (Ezra ch. 3) but was subsequently discontinued for eighteen years.

Haggai conveyed the following "In the seventh month [*Tishrei*] on the twenty first of the month [the seventh day of *Sukkot* — *Hoshana Rabbah* —] the word of Hashem came through Haggai the prophet saying ... for thus said Hashem, 'there will be one more; it is a small one, I will shake the heavens and the earth and the sea and the dry land'" (2:1,6).

The message of this prophecy was that in addition to the current subjugation under Persia, one more nation would subdue the Jews, the Greeks; but their domination would last only a short time (Rashi). Hashem was thus saying, "During the Greek rule, I will cause a major upheaval in the land" — a reference to the Hasmoneans revolt against the Greeks and the miracle of *Chanukah*.

(עי' רד"ק)

"חנוכה – סוכות"
"Chanukah — Sukkot"

QUESTION: Where in the *Gemara* do we find a connection between *Chanukah* and *Sukkot?*

ANSWER: The connection between *Chanukah* and *Sukkot* is also evident from the tractate of *Sukkah*. It begins with laws pertaining to the construction of a *Sukkah* and concludes with a story connected to Hellenistic Jews in the day of the Syrian-Greeks.

The final *Mishnah* in the tractate of *Sukkah* (56a) relates that, in the *Beit Hamikdash* there were 24 *mishmorot* — watches — of *Kohanim,* who each served during a different week. At the end of the week the incoming and outgoing watches would divide the *lechem hapanim* — show-bread — that stood on the table the entire week. Normally the incoming watch would divide it among themselves in the north of the Courtyard, while the outgoing watch would do so in the south. Also each watch had its own ring affixed to the floor in which the head of the animal was enclosed to hold it down during slaughter. Every watch also had its own alcove in which to store knives. An exception to this was the watch of Bilgah; they always divided their share of *lechem hapanim* in the southern side of the Courtyard. Their ring and alcove was permanently closed, forcing them to use another watch's ring and alcove and thus suffer embarrassment.

The concluding piece of *Gemara* (56b) explains that this was a punishment to the family Bilgah for the following incident: Once, Miriam, the daughter of one of the members of the watch of Bilgah, became an apostate and married an officer of one of the Greek kings. When the Greeks subsequently entered the Sanctuary in the days of Matityahu ben Yochanan, she scornfully kicked with her sandal on the top of the Altar and exclaimed "Wolf! Wolf! how long will you consume the money of Israel and you do not stand by them in a time of pressing need." (She compared the Altar on which two sheep of *Karban Tamid* are offered daily to a wolf that devours sheep.)

When the Sages heard of this, they punished the entire watch of Bilgah in three ways that would demean it in the eyes of all onlookers. To explain why all were punished because of Miriam's outrageous behavior, the *Gemara* says that it was based on the adage "The utterances of a child in public express the view of either his father or his mother." Thus, it was clear to the Sages that her contemptuous behavior was symptomatic of the corruption of her family.

It is said about Torah, "The end is joined with the beginning and the beginning with the end (*Sefer Yetzirah* 1:7, see *Likkutei Sichos* vol. 14, p. 25). Hence, it is not accidental but intentional, that the tractate *Sukkah* begins with laws of the *Sukkah* and ends with an incident in the days of Matityahu ben Yochanan, one of the heroes of *Chanukah*.

(שו"ת משנה שכיר)

* * *

Because of the relation of *Sukkot* and *Chanukah*, those who beautify their *Sukkah* with various items, also have a custom to hang up a bottle of oil.

(עי' נטעי גבריאל)

"סוכות – חנוכה – יעקב גאולה"

"Sukkot and Chanukah —
Yaakov and Redemption."

QUESTION: What is the connection between *Sukkot,* *Chanukah,* Yaakov and the coming redemption?

ANSWER: From a spiritual perspective *Chanukah* is eight days and we kindle eight candles because it has a connection with the *Ohr Haganuz* — *hidden light* — which will be revealed in its full glory in the days of *Mashiach* (see p. 17) and just as the number eight transcends the limits of creation which is associated with the seven days of the week and the seven orbital planets, so too, *Mashiach* is above *seder hishtalshelut* — chain of creation.

Just as *Chanukah* is celebrated for eight days, likewise, *Sukkot* is celebrated eight days. And there is actually a connection between the two (see page 125).

The three festivals, *Pesach, Shavuot* and *Sukkot* correspond to the three patriarchs, Avraham, Yitzchak and Yaakov (see *Tur, Orach Chaim* 417). In addition the first and second *Beit Hamikdash,* which were destroyed, and the third *Beit Hamikdash,* which we will have in the Messianic era and which will be perpetual, correspond to the three patriarchs. They all rendered a description of the site where the *Beit Hamikdash* stood. The description identified with Avraham is that it was a mountain, as the Torah (*Bereishit* 22:14) records "on the *mountain* Hashem is seen." The description found in connection with Yitzchak is that it was a field, as stated, "Yitzchak went out to pray in the *field*" (ibid. 24:14). Yaakov called it a house, as it is stated "He named that place" 'the *House* of Hashem' (28:19).

Avraham's "mountain" represents the first *Beit Hamikdash.* Hashem watched over it like a guard strategically stationed on top of a mountain. This protection, however, was not permanent and it was ultimately destroyed. The "field" of Yitzchak (which is an empty place) signifies the second *Beit Hamikdash,* which in contrast to the first was lacking in Divine Presence (*Yoma* 21b). The "house" of Yaakov symbolizes the third *Beit Hamikdash,* which will enjoy Divine Presence and protection that is permanent and complete like a house (see *Pesachim* 88a, and *Maharsha*).

This indicates that the concepts of ultimate redemption, *Mashiach,* and the third *Beit Hamikdash* have a special connection with the patriarch Yaakov, to whom *Sukkot* corresponds, and to *Chanukah* (which is associated with *Sukkot*).

(התוועדיות תשמ״ח ח״ב ע׳ 115)

* * *

QUESTION: Since in contemporary times a *shul* is a *Beit Hamikdash* in miniature (*Megillah* 29a), what is the significance of these three titles for a *shul?*

ANSWER: The majority of people are not mountain climbers. Even those who are, do it rarely. Going out to the fields (vacationing in the country) is done more frequently and by a larger number of people. Living in a home is something all people do and at all times. Yaakov emphasized that the *shul* should resemble a home — a place visited by all people and at all times.

(מצאתי בכתבי אבי הרב שמואל פסח ז״ל באגאמילסקי)

* * *

The less one carries the easier it is to climb a mountain. When going out to the fields (on vacations) people take along baggage and dwell in cottages. However, the living conditions do not compare to the comforts of one's personal home. Yaakov emphasized that the place of worship be treated like a home — elegantly furnished and beautified to the highest degree.

הדודאים נתנו ריח...
The *Dudaim* Emit a Fragrance...

"הדודאים נתנו ריח ועל פתחינו כל מגדים"

**"The *dudaim* (jasmine or violets) emit a
fragrance and at all our doors are
all precious fruits." (*Shir Hashirim* 7:14)**

QUESTION: According to the *Midrash* the statement "The *dudaim* emit a fragrance" is a reference to Reuvein (of whom it says "he found *dudaim* in the field" — [*Bereishit* 30:14] and who saved Yosef [by advising that he be thrown into the pit in the wilderness]. The statement "At our doors are all precious fruits" refers to *Chanukah* candles which are placed by the doorway of the house from the outside.

What is the *Midrash* conveying?

ANSWER: When the brothers saw Yosef from afar, they conspired to kill him. Reuvein said to them *"Al tishpechu dam"* — "Do not shed blood!" (ibid 37:22). According to the *Arizal* (in his *Siddur*), Reuvein warned them that if they were to shed his blood and kill him they would not merit the forty four candles of *Chanukah* (the word *"dam"* (דם) numerically equals forty four).

Hence, the *Midrash* is saying that thanks to Reuvein's intervention on behalf of Yosef today we have "precious fruits" — the 44 *Chanukah* candles — at our doorways.

(חתן סופר על עניני חנוכה)

Alternatively, a person once donated generously to the construction of a synagogue and requested that his name be placed over the entrance. The Board of Directors refused, arguing that charity should be performed discreetly and quietly. The issue was brought before the Rashba (Reb Shlomo ben Aderet) who ruled (Responsa, vol. I, #582, see *Rama, Yoreh Dei'ah* 249:13) that *"Mitzvah lefarseim otei mitzvah"*

— "It is a *mitzvah* to publicize the doers of a *mitzvah* (if they don't object and request anonymity)." He based his ruling on the *pasuk* in the Torah that states "and Reuvein heard and he rescued him from their hands" (ibid. 37:21), which shows that Torah is of the opinion that one should be publicly acknowledged for performing a good deed.

The purpose of lighting *Chanukah* candles at the doorway on the outside of one's house is to publicize the miracle of *Chanukah* and simultaneously publicize the good work of the Hasmoneans, thanks to whose dedication to Torah, Hashem's salvation was merited.

Hence, the *Midrash* is saying that we can derive an important insight from the *dudaim,* which emit fragrance, i.e. Reuvein, who is associated with *dudaim*, and whose good deed is recorded in the Torah for eternity. We thus learn that it is the proper thing to put "precious fruits at our door" — the *Chanukah* light on the outside — thereby publicizing the miracle which was brought through the righteous Hasmoneans.

(ברכת חיים בשם קול רנה)

"הדודאים נתנו ריח ועל פתחינו כל מגדים חדשים וגם ישנים"

"The *dudaim* emit a fragrance, at our doors are all precious fruits, new and old."

QUESTION: What are the precious new and old fruits at our doors?

ANSWER: The *Midrash* says that the statement "The *dudaim* emit a fragrance" is a reference to Reuvein of whom the Torah (*Bereishit* 30:14) says that "he found *dudaim* in the field," and the phrase "at our doors are all precious fruits" is a reference to the *Chanukah Menorah* which is kindled at the entrance door to the home.

Reuvein went out to the fields "in the days of the wheat harvest," which occurs in the month of *Sivan*. In the field he found *dudaim* and brought them to his mother, Leah. Rachel requested some of them, and in exchange she allowed Leah to spend the night with Yaakov. According to the Kabbalists, that night was the eve of *Shavuot,* and Yissachar was then conceived. Seven months later, on the 25th of *Kislev,* Yissachar was born. (The *Gemara* [*Rosh Hashanah* 11a] says that "one who gives birth at seven months, can give birth before the end of the seventh month.")

The men of the tribe of Yissachar were great Torah scholars and were "men with understanding for all times" (I Chronicles, 12:23). Thanks to Reuvein's *dudaim* we have Yissachar from whom the good aroma of Torah emits throughout the world. It was they who established *Chanukah* as a *Yom Tov,* as stated in the popular hymn *"Ma'oz Tzur,"* "Men with understanding, eight days established for song and jubilations."

According to *halachah,* the *mezuzah* should be placed on the right side of the door while the *Chanukah* lights should be placed on the left. *Mezuzah* is a *mitzvah* written in the Torah and *Chanukah* is a *mitzvah* which the Rabbis instituted. Thus, the *pasuk* is saying that thanks to Reuvein's *dudaim,* which brought about the birth of Yissachar, the aroma of Torah spreads throughout the world, and at our doors are all precious fruits new and old — the *mezuzah* of old and the newly ordained *Chanukah* lights, which the scholars of Yissachar instituted.

(בני יששכר)

רמזים ומנהגים
Hints and Customs

מנהגי חנוכה
Chanukah Customs

"חנוכה געלט"

"Chanukah Gelt — money"

QUESTION: What is the reason for the universally popular accepted custom of giving children *Chanukah* gelt?

ANSWER: The struggle between the brothers Yaakov and Eisav was not an ordinary family rivalry. It is a metaphor for the Jews in *Galut* — exile — and the struggles they encounter at the hands of the Monarchies who subjugate them. Likewise, the entire story of Yosef in Egypt is a metaphor for the Jews' going into exile, the persecutions they will suffer, and the ultimate redemption through *Mashiach,* when affluence will be bountiful, as the Rambam writes in his conclusion to *Mishnah Torah,* (*Melachim* 12:5).

When Eisav met Yaakov, he refused the gift that he had prepared for him, saying, *"Achi yehi lecha asher lach"* — "My brother, let yours be yours" (33:9). Why was the wicked Eisav suddenly so generous?

The *Midrash* (*Rabbah Bereishit* 78:12) says that "All the gifts which Yaakov gave to Eisav, the nations will return them to King *Mashiach."* Proof to this is in the verse "The kings of Tarshish and of the isles shall return tribute" (Psalms 72:10), it does not say, "shall bring," but *"shall return."* Hence, Eisav knew that this gift was something which would be his only temporarily and that it would have to be returned when *Mashiach* comes. Therefore, he said to Yaakov, "Since, in reality, this is destined to be yours, keep it and don't cause me the hardship of having to care for it and pay it back at a later date."

Likewise, when the brothers returned to Egypt and told the man [Menasheh] in charge of Yosef's household about their mysterious finding of their purchase money in their sacks. He said to them, "Do not worry... *kaspechem bah eilai* — your [payment] money reached me" ["Don't worry, I received your money"] (Ibid. 43:23).

The man in charge was Menasheh. Why did he lie?

Hashem told Avraham that the Jewish people would be slaves for 400 years in a strange land [Egypt], and afterwards they would go out with great wealth. According to the *Midrash,* the reason for the famine was to increase the wealth of Egypt, for the Jews were destined to eventually receive this wealth. (See *Yalkut Reuveini, Lech Lecha*)

Bearing this in mind, Menasheh told his uncles, "Whatever money I have taken in until now by selling grain to the entire world is in reality *your* money. Since all the money I receive from sales will ultimately be yours in the future, why should I bother now to take *your* money and later need to return it to you?"

In fact, immediately before the Jews left Egypt, Hashem instructed Moshe to tell the Jews that they should borrow from their Egyptian neighbors "silver vessels and gold vessels" (*Shemot* 11:2). Afterwards, they also obtained the Egyptian's wealth when they sank in the sea. All this was a part of the fulfillment of Hashem's promise to Avraham, "And afterwards they will leave with great wealth.

According to the *Gemara* (*Pesachim* 119a) the wealth the Jews amassed changed hands a few times. "It remained in Israel until the reign of Tzidkiyahu. Then the Chaldeans came and took it from Tzidkiyahu (when Nevuchadnetzar of Babylon exiled the Jewish people — II King, ch. 25). The Persians then came and took it from the Chaldeans (when they conquered Babylon — Daniel 5:27-6:1). The Greeks came and took it from the Persians (Alexander the Great conquered Persia — Josephus ch. 9). Ultimately, the Romans came and took the wealth from the hands of the Greeks and it still remains in Rome until today." When King *Mashiach* comes, all this wealth plus treasures which Yosef buried in Egypt (see *Tosafot* ibid.) will come back to the Jewish people.

Chanukah is a period of preparation for the days of *Mashiach* when we will enjoy the *Ohr haganuz* — the revelation of the hidden light (see p. 17). At that time Hashem will make His beloved children — the Jewish people — the beneficiaries of the world's wealth. Thus, to demonstrate our eager anticipation for the glorious period when Hashem will give His children *gelt* — money — we have the custom of giving our children and other Jewish children *Chanukah gelt*.

(עי' בית יעקב, בראשית - מסלתון, אוהל יעקב - המגיד מדובנא)

"נוהגין הנערים העניים לסבב בחנוכה על הפתחים"

"It is the custom of the poor young boys to go around to the doors on *Chanukah* [for *tzedakah*]." (*Magen Avraham* 670:1)

QUESTION: What is the reason for giving *tzedakah* on *Chanukah?*

ANSWER: The Syrian-Greeks wanted to detach the Jews from Torah study. In addition, according to a *Beraita* (see *Tur Orach Chaim* 670, *Bach*), because the Jews were lax in *Avodah* — serving Hashem — they were subject to a decree by the Syrian-Greeks to abolish the *karban Tamid* — daily sacrifice. When they repented and sacrificed their lives for the *Beit Hamikdash,* — which was the citadel of *Avodah,* their salvation came through the *Kohanim* — Hashem's servants in the *Beit Hamikdash.*

In commemoration, an eight-day festival was established with *Hallel* and *Hoda'ah* — reciting the *Hallel* and thanksgiving, which is basically prayer and which is considered *Avodah,* as the Gemara (*Ta'anit* 2a) says in regard to the Scriptural phrase *"Ule'avdo bechol levavechem"* — "And serve Him with all your heart" (*Devarim* 11:13) — that *avodah shebalev* — service performed in the heart — is prayer.

It is stated in *Pirkei Avot* (1:2) that the world stands on three pillars, Torah, *avodah* and *gemilut chassadim* — Torah study, service of Hashem and acts of kindness (charity). After their salvation, the Jews increased their study of Torah to counter the vile attempts of *lehashkicham Toratecha* — to make the Jews forget Your Torah — and added extra *avodah*-prayer (*Hallel vehoda'ah*) because of the Syrians' attempt to nullify the service of the *Beit Hamikdash*. Therefore, in keeping with the wisdom of King Shlomo that "a three ply cord is not easily severed" (*Kohelet* 4:12), it is also customary to increase in *tzedakah* which represents the third pillar on which the world stands — *gemilut chassadim* — charity.

(פרי מגדים)

"נוהגין הנערים העניים לסבב בחנוכה על הפתחים"

"It is the custom of the poor young boys to go around to the doors on *Chanukah* [for *tzedakah*]." (*Magen Avraham* 670:1)

QUESTION: Why the emphasis to go around to the *doors?*
ANSWER: There is a discussion in the *Gemara* (*Shabbat* 22a) concerning whether the *Chanukah Menorah* should be placed on the right or the left side of the doorway. The conclusion is that it should be placed on the left side so that it shall be *"Chanukah misemol"* — the *Chanukah* light on the left side — and *"mezuzah mimin"* — the *mezuzah* on the right.

The first letters of the words *"mezuzah yemin Chanukah semol"* (מזוזה ימין חנוכה שמאל) — *"mezuzah* on the right, *Chanukah* on the left" — spell the word *"Mashiach"* (משיח).

Now, there is a distance between the letters *mem-yud* and the letters *chet-shin* because they are the two extreme sides of the doorway. Therefore, the way to bring them close to each other and thus have *Mashiach* is through *tzedakah*, as the *Gemara* says (*Bava Batra* 10a), "Charity is great because it brings the redemption closer."

Hence, when the young boys go to the doorways for *Tzedakah* and the master of the house receives them generously, the merit of the *Tzedakah* unites the distanced *mem-yud* and *chet-shin,* leading to the speedy revelation of *Mashiach.*

(אור לשמים – ליקוטים, מר' מאיר הלוי זצ"ל מסטאבעניץ ואפטא)

"מרבים בצדקה בימי חנוכה"

"Charity should be dispensed liberally on *Chanukah.*" (*Kitzur Shulchan Aruch* 139:1)

QUESTION: What is the connection between giving charity on *Chanukah* and the miracle of the *pach* — flask — of oil?

ANSWER: When the angel who was Eisav's representative fought with Yaakov, the Torah relates that when he realized that he could not overcome him, *"vayiga bechaf yereicho"* — "he struck the hollow of his thighbone." The *Midrash* (Rabbah, Bereishit 77:4) says that this is a reference to the generations that emanate from the thigh of Yaakov.

The *Shelah* explains that the angel was referring to Yaakov's offspring — the tribes — whose iniquity is alluded to in the letters of the word *"chaf"* (כף), and the Hasmoneans ultimately corrected their iniquity by converting the *chaf* (כף) to *pach* — (פך).

This means the following: In the word *"chaf"* (כף) and also in the word *"pach"* (פך) there is the letter *chaf* (כ) and the letter *pei* (ף). The *chaf* stands for the *chaf [hayad]* — palm [of the hand] — which should be open to give *tzedakah,* and the *pei* is for the *peh* — mouth — which should be closed and not speak *lashon hara* — slander.

In the episode with Yaakov and the angel the *chaf* (כ) is closed from three sides and the [final] *pei* (ף) is open. The angel was alluding to the children of Yaakov, who engaged in *lashon hara* — slander — and who were greedy to have money for themselves, which is the opposite of opening the hand and giving away money to *tzedakah*. Of Yosef the *Torah* (*Bereishit* 37:2) writes, "And Yosef would bring evil reports of them to their father"; he slandered his brothers with his *mouth* to his father that they were violating Torah rules (see Rashi). The brothers were eager to have money in *their hands,* and thus "they sold Yosef to the Ishmaelites for twenty pieces of silver" (37:28).

The Hasmoneans, who found a *pach* [of oil], converted the order of the letters in the word *"chaf"* (כף) to *"pach"* (פך) in order to correct the iniquity of their predecessors. In the word *"pach"* the *pei* (פ) is closed and the *chaf* (ך) is open to allude that the righteous Hasmoneans under the leadership of Yehudah HaMacabee closed the mouths, i.e. killed the Hellenized Jews who joined the Syrian-Greeks and used their *mouths* to malign the Jews. These Jews also blasphemed Hashem and would inform the enemy about their Jewish brethren. The Hasmoneans also opened *their hands* and distributed much of the wealth they seized from the enemy to the poor and needy (see Josephus).

Hence, we commemorate the *tzedakah* of the Hasmoneans every *Chanukah* by intensifying this good trait and giving *tzedakah* with an open hand.

(של"ה פ' וישב דף ש"א ע"ב)

*   *   *

Incidentally, the numerical value of the words *"neis Chanukah"* (נס חנוכה) is 199, the same as the word *tzedakah* (צדקה). This indicates that when the miracle of *Chanukah* is celebrated, *tzedakah* should be given.

(ר' שלמה זצ"ל מבאבוב)

The numerical value of the word *tzedakah* (199) implies the following message:

The *Mishnah* (*Pei'ah* 8:8) says that one who has two hundred *zuz* (Talmudic currency) should not take any charity.

However, one with only one hundred and ninety-nine *zuz* who is given one thousand *zuz* at one time may take it.

The word *"tzedakah"* (צדקה) has the numerical value of one hundred and ninety-nine, which teaches us that as long as a person has no more than one hundred and ninety-nine, he may be a recipient.

(מהר"ל)

"סביבון – דריידל"
"Dreidel"

QUESTION: Sharp rebuke has been written against those who play various card games during *Chanukah* (see *Kedushat Levi*); nevertheless, the playing of *dreidel* is accepted in all circles. Why did it receive such acceptance?

ANSWER: The *dreidel* teaches us an eternal verity about the Jewish people, Hashem's chosen people, and it depicts their past, present and future.

When Hashem gave Avraham His blessing for children, He told him that they would be like the stars in heaven (*Bereishit* 16:5). And indeed, the Jewish people is like the heavenly stars. Just as the stars turn under Hashem's momentum, so has the Jewish people been "turning" for thousands of years. What a wonder it is to behold: More than once it has seemed that the feeble Jewish *dreidel* is about to fall. Babylonia, Greece, Rome, Spain, Russia, Poland, Germany all came and blew mightily on this pitifully small *dreidel* in an attempt to fell it, but Hashem always gave it another spin and the Jewish people leaped back to life, with renewed vigor and courage, virtually dancing, spinning more proudly, more energetically, than ever.

The *dreidel* has only one foot — one axis. It cannot stand at all; it can only spin. This has always been the situation of the Jews among the nations of the world. Throughout our exile we have spun on one foot; it was practically impossible for us to remain standing in one spot. We were without a foundation, without a soil, to stand on. Very often we even had no choice but to spin on our "heads," as a *dreidel* can be made to do — but we kept spinning away in what was virtually a feat of perpetual motion.

It even came into the language as an idiom. Asked how they were managing with respect to livelihood, Jews often answer: *"men dreid zich"* — "Oh, one keeps spinning."

It is different with the nations of the world. There have been great nations that have ruled mighty empires — but for how long? One after the other they have disappeared without a living trace. The nations of the world have been like *dreidels* spun by human hands — the hands of autocrats, despots, dictators and tyrants who made their countries great but only for a short while. A twist, a spin, and they faltered and fell.

The *dreidel* of the Jewish people is eternal because that is the way G-d created us and chose us to be. Weak, somewhat fragile, but we go on spinning forever — for so long as the world and the stars of the heavens go on spinning, so do the Jews on earth also continue to spin. It is Hashem who controls our spinning, and He makes sure that it be never-ending.

The Jewish *dreidel* has one of the Hebrew letter, *nun, gimmel, hei* and *shin* on each of its four sides. This stands for *neis gadol hayah sham* (נס גדול היה שם) — a great miracle took place there. Yes, throughout our history, wherever we sojourned our existence was a great miracle.

These letters — נ׳ ג׳ ה׳ ש׳ — add up to 358 which is also the numerical equivalent of the word *"Mashiach."* The significance of this is that the Final Redemption, the Messianic Redemption, will also be brought about by a twist of G-d's hand.

(From Prison to Pulpit, 1975 — הרב יצחק חיים שי׳ אביגדור)

"סביבון – דריידל"

"Dreidel"

QUESTION: What is the significance of the letters ג,ש,נ,ה, on the *dreidel*?

ANSWER: The four letters ג,ש,נ,ה represent the four Monarchies of the secular world who exiled the Jewish people and caused us anguish. The *"Gimmel"* is for Greece-Syria — who are headed by Gog (גוג). Yavan — Greece — was a descendant of *Yafet* son of Noach (*Bereishit* 10:2). Gog was from the land of Magog (a Yafet descendant) and was a king over families of Yafet (see Ezekiel ch. 38). The *"shin"* is for Sei'ir (שעיר), which represents Rome-Edom, as is stated (*Bereishit* 36:8-9) "Eisav settled on Mount Sei'ir — Eisav, he is Edom. And these are the descendants of Eisav, ancestor of Edom, on Mount Sei'ir." The *"nun"* is for Nevuchadnetzar (נבוכדנצר) the ruler of Babylon and the *"hei"* is for Haman (המן) of Media-Persia.

(ספר נרות שמונה)

* * *

The *dreidel* consists of a core — a central piece of wood — and each of the four pieces attached to it bears a letter representing one of the four Monarchies. It revolves on the central point that unites them all. The central point on which the entire world revolves is the Jewish nation. Ultimately, each side will fall and become nullified to the central point, which is the Jews. This will occur when גשנה — which has the numerical value of 358 (as does *Mashiach* [משיח]) will be revealed. At that time the prophecy will be fulfilled that "For then I will change the nations [to speak] a pure language [they will no longer speak of idols] so that they will proclaim the Name of Hashem, to worship Him with a united resolve" (Zephaniah 3:9).

When the revelation of *Mashiach* (358) will occur, the glory of Hashem will be in its fullest measure and all will recognize and declare that "י-ה-ו-ה מלך, י-ה-ו-ה מלך, י-ה-ו-ה- ימלך"

— "Hashem is the King, Hashem was the King and Hashem will be the King." This statement, too, has the numerical value of 358.

Thus, on the festival of *Chanukah*, which is a *chinuch* — preparation — to the coming redemption, the *dreidel* has a special significance. It emphasizes that the great miracle we are anticipating is the coming of *Mashiach*, who will ultimately unite the entire world to serve Hashem.

(בני יששכר מאמרי חודש כסלו טבת מאמר ב)

"סביבון – דריידל"
"*Dreidel*"

QUESTION: Why on *Chanukah* do we play with a *dreidel* and on *Purim* we use a *gragger*?

ANSWER: The miracle of *Chanukah* was above the laws of nature. The Jewish people were the minority and the Greeks were the majority; we were the weak and they were the strong. Nevertheless, thanks to heavenly intervention, the miracle took place and the Jews were the victors.

On *Purim*, the miracle was clothed entirely within the laws of nature. The Jewish people gathered in prayer and fasting. Esther pleaded their case before the king. Out of love for his Queen, he killed Haman — her arch enemy.

Since the miracle of *Chanukah* came down from above (אתערותא דלעילא), we spin the *dreidel* with the handle on top. The miracle of *Purim* was through an awakening from below (אתערותא דלתתא) — consequently we turn the *gragger* with the handle below.

(קרבן העני)

"סביבון – דריידל"
"*Dreidel*"

QUESTION: Where is there a hint in the Torah for playing *dreidel* on *Chanukah*?

ANSWER: *Chanukah* always falls out in the week of
Parshat Mikeitz. When the brothers were brought to Yosef's
home and they did not know that it was for a meal, they were
frightened and they said "Because of the money replaced in
our saddlebags earlier are we being brought *lehitgoleil aleinu* —
to bring a charge against us — and to cast [libel] down upon
us" (*Bereishit* 43:18). Rashi explains the word *"lehitgoleil"*
literally: "to be rolled." Thus, they were saying "We are being
brought, 'for the false charge about the money to be *rolled*
upon us.'"

The expression containing the word *"lehigoleil"* — "to be
rolled" — is superfluous since they also said "and to cast
[libel] down upon us." Perhaps they expressed themselves
this way to allude that during this week there will be much
"rolling" of the *dreidel*.

"יש אומרים שיש לאכול גבינה בחנוכה לפי שהנם נעשה בחלב
שהאכילה יהודית את האויב"

**"Some say that cheese should be eaten on
Chanukah because the miracle occurred thanks
to the dairy that Yehudit fed the enemy."
(*Orach Chaim*, 670:2)**

QUESTION: The oppressors had decreed that a maiden
before her marriage must first cohabit with the Governor, but
the daughter of Yochanan the *Kohen Gadol* outwitted him. She
was a very beautiful woman, and she reluctantly pretended to
accede to the request of the head oppressor. She prepared
dishes of cheese for him, which made him thirsty. He then
drank wine, became intoxicated, and fell asleep — whereupon
she cut off his head and brought it to Jerusalem. Finding that
their commander was dead, the armies became panicky and
fled (*Mishnah Berurah*).

Since nothing is accidental and everything is a part of
Divine Providence, why is the miracle of the *Chanukah* victory
connected particularly with milk?

ANSWER: On the first day of *Shavuot* it is customary to eat a dairy meal. One of the explanations given for this custom is based on a *Midrash* (*Shochar Tov,* Psalm 8) that when Moshe came up to heaven to receive the Torah, the angels objected, claiming "keep your glory in heaven." They wanted the Torah for themselves and opposed its being given away to humans. Hashem told them, "How can you request the Torah if you violated it when you visited the house of Avraham to inform him of the forthcoming birth of Yitzchak? The Torah forbids the eating of meat with milk, and the Torah says 'He took cream and milk and the calf that he prepared, and placed these before them, and they ate'" (*Bereishit* 18:8).

Consequently, we received the Torah and not the angles because of the milk they ate together with the meat. Therefore, on the first day of *Shavuot,* which commemorates our receiving the Torah, we eat a dairy meal.

The Greek-Syrians intended to stop the Jews from studying Torah so that it would be forgotten, and their plan was nullified with the victory of the Hasmoneans. Thus, in a sense, *Chanukah* is the day when Torah was again given to the Jewish people. Hence, there is a parallel between *Chanukah* and *Shavuot:* on both occasions we received the Torah thanks to milk, and on both holidays we commemorate this by eating cheese and dairy products.

(בני יששכר, וע״י סדר הדורות ג״א תרכ״ב)

רמזים לחנוכה בפרשיות
וישב, מקץ, ויגש
Hints for *Chanukah* in
Vayeishev, Mikeitz, Vayigash

"אלה תולדות יעקב, יוסף"

"These are the offspring of Yaakov: Joseph."
(37:2)

QUESTION: What is the solution to the following riddle? Take what Yosef found, add to it his garments, then add to it his sale and add to this what was added to him, and you have *Chanukah*.

ANSWER: The Torah (*Bereishit* 39:4) says of Yosef that "*vayimtza Yosef chein*" — "Yosef found favor [in his — Potiphar's — eyes]."

When Paroah appointed Yosef as viceroy, it says "*veyalbeish oto bigdei sheish*" — "he dressed him in garments of fine linen" (41:42).

Yosef was sold to the Ishmaelites "*b'esrim Kesef*" — "for twenty pieces of silver" (37:28).

The *Gemara* (*Sotah* 10a) says that because Yosef sanctified the Name of Heaven in seclusion (he succeeded in withstanding Potiphar's wife's attempt to seduce him in the privacy of her home — ibid., 39:11,12), he merited that the letter "*hei*" from Hashem's Name be added to his name, as it is written (Psalms 81:6), "*eidut beyhosef samo*" (עדות ביהוסף שמו) — "He made a testimony for Yosef" [when he went out over the land of Egypt — his name is spelled with an extra "*hei*"].

If you take the *chein* — favor — that Yosef found   חן

add to it his garments — *sheish* — (שש), which in Hebrew also

means six and the Hebrew numeral for six is *vav* —   ו

Add to this his sale, *esrim* — twenty —   כ

Finally add what was added to his name —   ה

———

חנוכה

You have the word *"Chanukah"* in the name of Yosef, and it is all in the Torah portion of *Vayeishev* and *Mikeitz* the weeks when *Chanukah* occurs.

(ר׳ אברהם שמחה זצ״ל מבאראנוב)

"ויחלם יוסף חלום" – "ויהי מקץ שנתים ימים ופרעה חלם"

"Yosef dreamt a dream" — "At the end of two years Paroah was dreaming." (37:5, 41:1)

The *Al Hanissim* prayer states that the miracle of *Chanukah* was that "the many were delivered into the hand of few" and "the strong into the hand of the weak." This thought is emphasized in the *parshiot* of *Vayeishev* and *Mikeitz*. In *Parshat Vayeishev* we read about Yosef's dreams, and in the *Parshat Mikeitz* we read about Paroah's dreams. In Paroah's dreams the weak conquer the strong. Yosef dreamt that the majority can be subordinate to the minority. Thus, the common denominator of both dreams is that quantity or strength is not necessarily the decisive factor.

(ברכת חיים)

* * *

Alternatively, in *Parshat Vayeishev* we read about Yosef's coming to visit his brothers when they are pasturing the sheep. The Torah relates that "They saw him from afar... they conspired toward him to kill him... Reuvein said to them 'Do not shed blood! Throw him into the pit in the wilderness, but lay no hand upon him!'" (37:18, 22). Here is an example of the few prevailing over the many. Reuvein, the minority opinion, stood up against his brothers the majority, and they acquiesced.

In *Parshat Mikeitz* after all the wise men were unable to interpret Paroah's dream, he called on the poor slave Yosef. Regardless of the fact that Paroah declared himself a god and the people accepted him as such (See *Shemot* 7:15, Rashi), four times, Yosef fearlessly declared in their presence the omnipotence of Hashem: 1) "That is beyond me, Hashem will respond to Paroah's welfare" (41:16). 2) "What Hashem is doing He told to Paroah" (41:26). 3) "What Hashem is doing He has shown to Paroah" (41:28). 4) "It is because the matter stands ready before Hashem and Hashem is hastening to do it" (41:32).

Yosef, the minority, stood valiantly in front of Paroah and his people and prevailed. Paroah was so impressed by the faith and conviction of this individual Jew that he himself was forced to recognize Hashem as one and only G-d, as the Torah relates, "He said to his servants, 'can we find one such as this — a man in whom is the spirit of *Hashem?*' Then he said to Yosef, 'Since *Hashem* had informed you all of this, there is no one so discerning and wise as you'" (41:38, 39). Paroah proceeded to appoint Yosef as viceroy, and *all* yielded to the *single* Yosef.

(הגיוני הלכה - הרב יצחק מירסקי)

*   *   *

In the olden days debates would take place between priests and Rabbis. The priests would attempt to prove the correctness of their faith and force the Jews to convert. Once, a priest asked a rabbi, "Since we are the majority and you are the minority, why don't you obey what it says in your Torah 'follow the majority' (*Shemot* 23:2) and join our religion?"

The rabbi wisely responded, "The law of following the majority applies only when there is doubt. However, though we are a minority, we Jews have no doubts about our faith

and are convinced that our G-d is the one and only G-d and
Master of the entire world."

(אוצר חיים)

"ויהי מקץ שנתים ימים"

"And it came to pass at the end of two full years." (41:1)

According to *halachah*, the *Menorah* is placed on the left
side of the doorpost, opposite the *mezuzah*, which is on the
right. In the *pasuk* "ויהי מקץ שנתים," the word "שנתים" is an
acronym for שמאל נרות תדליק, ימין מזוזה (On the left kindle the
candles, on the right place the *mezuzah*).

(שלטי הגבורים)

"וחמש את ארץ מצרים"

"And he shall prepare the land of Egypt." (41:34)

During Yaakov's confrontation with the angel, it says that
the angel struck *"kaf yereicho"* — "the socket of his hip"
(*Bereishit* 32:26). The *Midrash* explains that this is a reference
to his children (the children of Yaakov are referred to as
"yotzei yereicho" — "those that came out of his thigh" (ibid.
46:26). The angels' complaint was that Yaakov vowed "All
that You will give me, I shall repeatedly tithe to You" (ibid.
28:22), and he never tithed his children. In response, Yaakov
immediately designated Levi as a tithe of his children to be
dedicated to the service of Hashem. Since he said *"aseir
a'asrenu"* — which means two times *ma'aseir* — i.e. one fifth
— he then also tithed his son Yissachar to Hashem as one to
be dedicated entirely to Torah study.

The vile desires of the Syrian-Greeks to defile the *Beit
Hamikdash* and to cause the forgetting of Torah mostly
affected the tribe of Levi, the *Kohanim* and *Levites* who did the
service in the *Beit Hamikdash*, and the tribe of Yissachar, who
were totally immersed in Torah study. Thus, the victory was
mostly felt by those who represented the one fifth (20%)
which Yaakov tithed to Hashem. The Levites now returned to

their service in the *Beit Hamikdash* and the tribe of Yissachar freely immersed themselves in Torah study without any interference.

The connection of *Chanukah* and *Parshat Mikeitz* is that the importance of double tithing — giving one fifth — was popularized by Yosef in this *Parshah*. When he came before Paroah, he told him that a famine was coming and advised that *"vechimeish et Eretz Mitzraim"* — "he shall prepare the land of Egypt" (41:34). According to *Targum Yonatan ben Uziel,* the word *"vechimeish"* means that 1/5 of the produce was to be taken from the people for the king's coffers during the seven years of abundance

(בני יששכר – בענין מעשר הבנים עי׳ תרגום יונתן בן עוזיאל בראשית ל״ב:כ״ה
ובענין החומש עי׳ פני דוד להחיד״א פ׳ בהעלותך)

"וחמש את ארץ מצרים"

"And he shall prepare the land of Egypt." (41:34)

According to the *Midrash*, the Syrians-Greeks forbade the Jews to have a calendar based on the lunar system so that they would be unable to observe *Rosh Chodesh.* They also wanted the Jews to cease observing *milah* — circumcision — and *Shabbat.* The word *"chimeish"* (חמש) — "prepare" — is an acronym for these three edicts. The *"chet"* is for *"Chodesh"* (חודש) — month — the *"mem"* is for *"milah"* (מילה) — circumcision — and the *"shin"* is for *Shabbat* (שבת).

These three *mitzvot* are conduits for Hashem's presence to be among the Jewish people. Circumcision makes the Jews a receptacle to attain G-dliness, as is seen from Avraham, the first Jew to be circumcised. After Avraham circumcised himself, Hashem appeared to him with the angels of His chariot.

Of *Shabbat* the Torah (*Shemot* 31:16) says, "To make the *Shabbat ledorotam"* (לדרתם) — "for the generations." The *Zohar* says that since the word is written without a ו it can thus be read as *"lediratam"* — "for their dwelling" — an indication that Hashem establishes a dwelling among the Jews on *Shabbat*.

The Jewish calendar is based on the moon. Each month when we bless the new moon, it is tantamount to greeting the Divine presence. As stated in the prayer recited during the sanctifying of the moon, "Had Israel been privileged only to greet the countenance of their Father in Heaven once each and every month, it would have sufficed them" (*Sanhedrin* 42a).

Cognizant of what these *mitzvot* accomplish, Yosef wanted to make sure that even when the Jews would be in exile, Hashem's presence should be in their midst. Therefore, as the first Jew to go into exile, he paved the way for them by putting a special emphasis on observing the three *mitzvot* hinted in the word *"chimeish"* (חמש).

(ראש דוד להחיד"א וע"י בני יששכר חדש כסלו מאמר י"ג)

It is interesting to note that from Yosef's descent to Egypt until the Jews left Egypt there was a total of 232 years. (The interval from Yaakov's coming to Egypt until the redemption was 210 years, and Yosef was separated from Yaakov for 22 years.)

The numerical value of the words *"Yehi ohr"* (יהי אור) — "Let there be light" (*Bereishit* 1:3) — is 232. Thanks to Yosef's efforts for 232 years in behalf of these three *mitzvot* to assure that the Divine presence was with the Jewish people while they are in exile, they merited years later that *"Yehi ohr"* — "Let there be light" — the light of *Chanukah*. (See p. 158 for a connection between *Yehi ohr* and *Chanukah*.)

(See p. 158 for a connection between *Yehi ohr* and *Chanukah*.)

(בני יששכר)

"שבו שברו לנו מעט אכל"
"Go back buy us some food." (43:2)

A hint to forty-four [candles] is in Yaakov's command to his sons, *"Shuvu shibru lanu me'at ochel"* — "Go back, buy us some food" (43:2).

The word *"lanu"* (לנו) has the numerical value of eighty-six. The word *"shibru"* (שברו) also means to break. Thus, Yaakov was telling them *"shibru lanu"* — "break the word *'lanu'* [in half], and add to the half (forty-three) *'me'at ochel'* — the numerical value of the letter *'alef'* (א) which is *'me'at'* — least in numerical value among the letters of the word *'ochel'* (אכל)" — the total is forty-four.

(פרדס יוסף בשם אוהל מועד ח"א)

"וטבח טבח והכן"

"Slay an animal and prepare it." (43:16)

According to some opinions (*Orach Chaim* 670:2), it is proper to have a festive meal on *Chanukah*. A hint for this may be found in Yosef's telling the overseer of his household *"Utevo'ach tevach vehachein"* (וטבח טבח והכן) — "Slay an animal and prepare it, for these men shall dine with me at noon" (*Bereishit* 43:16). The words "וטבח טבח" have the numerical value of 44. During the eight days of *Chanukah* we kindle a total of 44 candles, including the *shamashim*.

(בשמים ראש)

Moreover in the expression of *tevach vehachein* (טבח והכן) — a slaying and prepare — the letter ח' of the word *tevach* (טבח) together with the letters of the word *vehachein* (והכן), spell the word *Chanukah*.

(תנא דבי אליהו)

"להתגלל עלינו"

"To bring a charge against us" (43:18)

The brothers expressed the fear that their being brought to Yosef's home was *"lehitgoleil aleinu"* — "so that a charge can be fabricated against us" (43:18). According to Rashi, the word *"lehitgoleil"* (להתגולל) literally means to *roll* [upon us an accusation]. They used this expression to indicate that there would come a time when it would be customary to *roll* the *dreidel* during the week of *Parshat Mikeitz*.

(ברכת חיים)

"ותרב משאת בנימן ממשאת כלם חמש ידות"

"And Binyamin's portion was greater than the portions of all of them fivefold." (43:34)

In the *Al Hanissim* prayer, the word *"yad"* — "hand" — is mentioned five times: *"Masarta giborim beyad chalashim, verabim beyad me'atim, utemei'im beyad tehorim, ureshaim beyad tzaddikim, vezeidim beyad oskei Toratecha"* — "You delivered the mighty into the hand of the weak, the many into the hand of the few, the impure into the hand of the pure, the wicked into the hand of the righteous, and wanton sinners into the hand of those who occupy themselves with Your Torah." A hint for this may be found in the *pasuk* "Binyamin's portion was *chameish yadot* — *five hands* (times) — as much as theirs" (43:34).

(ר' נפתלי מראפשיץ זצ"ל)

* * *

It is possible that the festive meal to which Yosef invited his brothers was also in honor of *Chanukah*. At the meal, when Yosef alluded to the five hands, he intended a message for his brothers.

There is a difficulty in the wording of this prayer. Grammatically it should be plural and read *"bidei"* — "in the hands" — and not the singular *"beyad"* — "in the hand."

Indeed, more than one hand fought in defense of the Jewish people. However, the secret of their success was the unity of the Hasmoneans. When members of a minority are united, they can easily conquer any power that seeks to destroy them.

Yosef was suggesting to his brothers that disaster occurs when unity is lacking. However, when we are united, we are the most powerful force in the world.

"קמ"ו פסוקים"

"There are 146 *pesukim* in *Parshat Mikeitz*."

QUESTION: Why necessarily 146?

ANSWER: The names of Hashem are an expression of His attributes. The holy four letter Name the Tetragramaton (י-ה-ו-ה) connotes *Rachamim* — Mercy. The Name *E-l* (א-ל) connotes *Chesed* — kindness, as King David says (Psalms 52:3) *"Chesed E-l kol hayom"* — "The kindness of Hashem is all day long."

According to Kabbalists, the miracles of *Chanukah* were a result of the manifestation of the two holy Names the Tetragramaton and *E-l* (representing His infinite Mercy and Kindness). The miracle expressed itself in the eight-day kindling of the seven candles of the *Menorah* — a total of 56 candles. This is alluded to in the verse *"E-l Y-H-V-H, vaya'er lanu"* — "G-d A-donai, He illuminated for us" (Psalms 118:27). The word *"lanu"* (לנו) contains a *nun-vav*, which numerically adds up to 56. Thus, the verse is saying that thanks to His attributes of Mercy and Kindness, as expressed in the Names *E-l* and *Havaye*, He miraculously illuminated *Lanu* — the נ"ו — 56 lights. (*"Lanu"* can be read as *"L'nun-vav,"* to the 56).

The word *"Chanukah"* (חנוכה) together with the two Holy Names (א-ל, י-ה-ו-ה) add up to 146. As a hint that the miracles of *Chanukah* were effectuated by His Holy Names, the *Parshah* in which *Chanukah* always occurs contains a total of 146 *pesukim*.

(בני יששכר)

"ותיבות אלפים כ"ה"

"There are 2025 words in *Parshat Mikeitz*."

Throughout the Torah, the number of *pesukim* in the *parshah* is written at the end of every *parshah*.

At the end of *Parshat Mikeitz*, besides the number of *pesukim*, we are also told that the *parshah* contains 2,025 words.

Why is it necessary to know the amount of words?

Parshat Mikeitz is usually read during the week of *Chanukah*. The 2,025 words in the *parshah* can serve as a hint for the *Yom Tov* of *Chanukah*. During *Chanukah* we light candles for eight nights. The *mitzvah* can be fulfilled with only one candle each night for the entire household.

In Hebrew the word for candle is *"neir"* (נר) which has the numerical value of 250. Eight times 250 equals 2,000. The event of lighting candles starts on the 25th day in the month of *Kislev*. Thus, 2,025 alludes to the 25th of *Kislev* and eight candles.

(תורה תמימה)

"אדני שאל את עבדיו לאמר היש לכם אב או אח:
ונאמר אל אדני יש לנו אב זקן"

"My lord asked his servants, saying: Have you a father, or a brother? And we said to my lord: We have an old father." (44:19-20)

The eight days of *Chanukah* usually extend into the week of *Vayigash*, and we learn about the brothers confronting Yosef, *"Adoni sha'al et avadav leimor hayeish lachem av o ach? Venomar el adoni: yeish lanu av zakein."* "My lord asked his servants, saying: Have you a father, or a brother? And we said to my lord: We have an old father."

This dialogue gives a hint about *Chanukah*:

In the *Gemara* (*Shabbat* 21b), *Beit Hillel* is of the opinion that on the first night of *Chanukah* one candle is lit, and each following night an additional candle. *Beit Shammai* is of the opinion that on the first night eight candles are lit, decreasing by one each succeeding night.

The brothers told Yosef, "You asked us, היש לכם' — 'are you of the opinion that' — 'אבי — 'we go from one (א) to two (ב) and so on, or' — 'אחי — 'on the (א) first night we light eight (ח) candles.' We replied יש לנו' — 'our custom is' — 'אבי — 'to increase from one to two because' — 'זקן — 'this is the opinion of the *father* of the school who was known as' — 'הלל הזקן' — 'Hillel the elder.' "

(נרות שמונה)

רמזים לחנוכה בתורה
Hints for *Chanukah* in the Torah

"א, ב... ת"
"*Alef Beit... Taf.*"

The entire *alef-beit*, comprising the letters with which the Torah was written, is a hint to *Chanukah* and some of its major laws.

The first eight letters (א׳ב׳ג׳ד׳ה׳ו׳ז׳ח׳) add up to 36. During the eight days of *Chanukah* we kindle a total of 36 candles (excluding the *shamashim*).

The letter ט׳ is a hint that the *Menorah* should be placed less than 10 *tefachim* (handbreadths) off the ground.

The letters י׳כ׳ stand for "*Yud kasher*" (י כשר) — 10 *tefachim* [and more is also] *kasher*.

However, the letters ל׳מ׳נ׳ס׳ע׳פ׳ stand for "*Lema'alah mei'esrim, neir, sukkah, eiruv, pesulah*" (למעלה מעשרים, נר, סוכה, עירוב, פסולה) — Above 20 [*amah*-cubits] a *neir*-candle, *sukkah*, and *eiruv*-crossbeam to enclose the entrance to a public area — are disqualified.

Finally, the letters צ׳ק׳ר׳ש׳ת׳ teach that "*Tzorech kedushah ra'u shamash tosif*" (צורך קדושה ראוי שמש תוסיף) — "because of the holiness of the candles [which may not be used for personal needs], it is proper that a *shamash* be added."

(עטרת זקנים סי׳ תרע״א – מדבר קדמות)

"יהי אור"
"Let there be light." (*Bereishit 1:3*)

The *Midrash* (*Bereishit Rabbah* 2:4) says that the phrase "And darkness [on the face of the abyss (1:2)]" symbolizes Greece, which darkened the eyes of the Jewish people with its decrees, ordering Israel "write on the horn of an ox that you have no portion in the G-d of Israel," i.e. Antiochus requested from the Jews a public disclaimer of Hashem and Torah.

Immediately following this the Torah says, "And G-d said "*Yehi ohr*" — "Let there be light" (1:3). The word "*ohr*" — "light" — is the twenty fifth word of the Torah. Moreover, the word "*yehi*" (יהי) — "let there be" — numerically adds up to twenty five. All this alludes that the darkness caused by the Greeks will be illuminated with the light (of the *Menorah*), which will be kindled by the Jews on the 25th [of *Kislev*].

(מהר"ל – הגר"א)

"וכל יתדות החצר נחשת. ואתה תצוה את בני ישראל
ויקחו אליך שמן זית זך כתית למאור להעלות נר תמיד"

"All the pegs of the courtyard of copper. And you will command the Children of Israel, that they shall take for you pure olive oil... to kindle a lamp continually." (*Shemot* 26:19-20)

QUESTION: What is the connection between the word "*nechoshet*" — "copper" — the final word of *Parshat Terumah*, with the command in the beginning of *Parshat Tetzaveh* to prepare pure olive oil for illumination?

Answer: King Nevuchadnetzar of Babylon had a very frightening dream which agitated him greatly. Afterwards, he forgot the details and thus did not know the dream's interpretation until Daniel told him that he had dreamt of an image whose head was of fine gold, with its breast and arms of silver, its belly and thighs of copper, and its legs of iron — and then all the parts crumbled together.

Daniel then interpreted all this as a reference to the four Monarchies who subjugated the Jewish people. The gold represented Nevuchadnetzar and his kingdom because of their tremendous power. The Persians and Medes were the silver. The copper kingdom was the Greek empire of Alexander the Great and his successors. (This includes Antiochus who was Macedonian and a descendant of Alexander the Macedonian.) Finally, the Roman empire dominated by Edom and Ishmael (represented by Christianity and Islam) are compared to the iron. Ultimately, they will all crumble under the kingdom of Hashem, which will be ruled by *Mashiach* (Daniel 2:31-45).

The last word of *Parshat Terumah*, *"nechoshet"* — "copper"
— would be a reference to the Syrian-Greek empire. The
Torah follows this up with the statement "Now you shall
command the Children of Israel that they shall take for you
pure olive oil to kindle the lamp continually" (27:20). The
Torah is hinting that in the days of the Greek empire
(*nechoshet* — copper) there will be a special need for pure
olive oil to kindle the *Menorah*.

(בני יששכר)

Incidentally, the word *"nechoshet"* (נחשת) is also an
acronym for *"Neir Chanukah sham tadliku"* (נר חנוכה שם תדליקו)
— *"Chanukah* candle there you will kindle."

The word *"nechoshet"* (נחשת) is an acronym for *"neir
Chanukah semol tadlik"* (נר חנוכה שמאל תדליק) — "Kindle the
Chanukah light on the left."

"Nechoshet" (נחשת) is also an acronym for *"Neir Chanukah
shamas tadlik"* (נר חנוכה שמש תדליק) — "For the candle of
Chanukah light a *shamash*."

This is followed with "And you shall command the
Children of Israel that they take pure olive oil" to indicate
that olive oil is most preferable for the kindling of the
Chanukah Menorah, which is placed on the left side of the
doorway, with a *Shamash* above.

(מטה משה, רוקח, הגהות מרדכי החדש)

"צו את בני ישראל ויקחו אליך שמן זית זך... להעלת נר תמיד...
על המנרה הטהרה יערך את הנרות"

**"Command the Children of Israel to take for you pure
olive oil... to kindle a lamp continually... on the pure
Menorah shall he arrange the lamps." (*Vayikra* 24:2, 4)**

In this *parshah* there is the following hint for *Chanukah*: In
the preceding *pesukim* there is a listing of all the Jewish *Yomim
Tovim* — Festivals — celebrated throughout the year. The
order in which they are mentioned is as follows: *Shabbat,
Pesach, Shavuot, Rosh Hashanah, Yom Kippur* and *Sukkot.*
Immediately following this the Torah continues, "Hashem said
to Moshe: 'Command the Children of Israel that they take to
you pure olive oil, pressed for lighting, to kindle a continual

lamp.'" This is a hint to *Chanukah*, which follows *Sukkot* on the calendar, and in which using olive oil is the most preferable way to fulfill the *mitzvah* (see *Orach Chaim* 673:1).

The Torah portion begins with the words *"Tzav et B'nei Yisrael"* (צו את בני ישראל) — "Command the Children of Israel" — which have the numerical value of 1,100, the same numerical value (*im hakolel* — counting the entire statement as one) as *"bimei Matityahu ben Yochanan"* (בימי מתתיהו בן יוחנן) — "in the day of Matityahu son of Yochanan".

Thus, the Torah is alluding that in the days of Matityahu son of Yochanan there will be a festival (*Chanukah*) following *Sukkot* when Jews will use pure olive oil to kindle the *Menorah*.

(רוקח – בני יששכר)

"צו את בני ישראל ויקחו אליך שמן זית זך... להעלת נר תמיד...
על המנרה הטהרה יערך את הנרות"

"Command the Children of Israel to take pure olive oil... to kindle a lamp continually... on the pure *Menorah* shall he arrange the lamps." (*Vayikra* 24:2, 4)

QUESTION: Why was Moshe first told to take pure olive oil *"leha'alot neir tamid"* — "to kindle a continual lamp" — in singular, and then it continues "on the pure *Menorah ya'aroch et haneirot* — "shall he arrange the lamps" — in plural?

ANSWER: According to some commentaries (see Avudraham), the word *"Chanukah"* is an acronym for *"Chet neirot vehalachah keBeit Hillel"* (ח' נרות והלכה כבית הלל) — "Kindle eight candles and the *halachah* is like *Beit Hillel*," alluding that on the first night one begins by lighting one candle and every night one adds a candle until the eighth night, when eight candles are lit.

Since this *parshah* is a hint to *Chanukah*, (see above) first it says *"neir"* — "candle" — in singular because at the start — the first night — only a single candle is lit. And henceforth, on each succeeding night, there are *neirot*, a plural number of candles, from two to eight.

(רוקח)

"כף אחת עשרה זהב מלאה קטרת"

"One gold ladle of ten (shekels) filled with incense..." (7:14)

During the entire *Yom Tov* of *Chanukah*, we read each morning about the offerings the *Nesi'im* brought to the dedication of the Altar. Among the donated items was "כף אחת עשרה זהב מלאה קטרת" — "One golden ladle filled with incense." These words are acronyms which allude to the basic laws of *Chanukah*.

כף = **כ**' **פחות** — The *Menorah* should be lower than 20 cubits above the ground.

אחת = **א-ח תדליק** — Kindle, starting with one and increase to eight.

עשרה = **עד שתכלה רגל השוק** — It may be lit until the passersby have vanished from the market.

זהב = **זמנה בין השמשות** — Lighting time starts at twilight.

מלאה = **מצותה להניחה אצל הפתח** — It should be placed near the entrance door.

קטרת = **קרוב טפח רוחב תדליק** — Within a handbreadth of the width of the door, kindle.

(פנינים יקרים)

קריאת התורה לימי חנוכה
Torah Reading for *Chanukah*

"נשיא אחד ליום נשיא אחד ליום יקריבו את קרבנם"

**"One leader each day, one leader each day shall
they bring their offering." (*Bamidbar* 7:11)**

QUESTION: There is a *Midrash pli'ah* (wondrous *Midrash*),
which says that "from here it is derived that the offerings of
the *nesi'im* were also brought on *Shabbat*." What in this *pasuk*
indicates that?

ANSWER: The dedication of the Altar started on the first
day of the month of *Nissan*, which that year happened to be a
Sunday (see *Shabbat* 87b). In all, there were a total of twelve
nesi'im bringing offerings. Should they not have been
permitted to bring their offerings on *Shabbat*, then the twelve
offerings would have extended over two weeks, and on every
weekday of the first week there would be a different *nasi*
offering for a total of six, and the same for every weekday of
the following week. Thus, over the two-week period, two
nesi'im would bring offerings on the two Sundays, two on the
two Mondays etc.

However, with offerings occurring on *Shabbat*, the
dedication would be completed in twelve days. Thus, in the
first week seven *nesi'im* would bring their offerings with the
remaining five offering on the first five days of the second
week, and Friday and *Shabbat* would be the only days to fall
once during this period and thus only one *nasi* would bring an
offering on these days.

Carefully analyzing our *pasuk*, the *Midrash* finds a difficulty
in the fact that the words *"nasi echad layom"* — "one *nasi* per
day" — are repeated. Therefore, the *Midrash* concludes that it is
not a redundancy, but intentionally phrased to teach us that on
two of the days (Friday and *Shabbat*) only one *nasi* offered,
while two *nesi'im* offered on all the other days which all fell

twice during the 12-day period. Hence, we can conclude that the offerings were also brought on *Shabbat*, since one *Shabbat* occurred during the twelve-day period.

(פנינים יקרים)

"ויהי המקריב ביום הראשון את קרבנו...ביום השני...ביום השלישי..."

"The one who brought his offering on the first day...on the second day...on the third day...."
(7:12, 18, 24)

QUESTION: Every day from *Rosh Chodesh* through the twelfth of *Nissan*, the section is read describing the offering brought by the *nasi* on that day (see *Ba'eir Heitav, Orach Chaim* 629:6), followed by a mystical prayer, *"Yehi Ratzon"* — "May it be Your will...." In it we say, "If I, Your servant, am of the tribe of (name of the tribe of that day) the Torah section of whose *nasi* I have recited today, then may all the 'holy sparks' and all the 'holy lights' which are contained in this tribe shine upon me."

How is it possible that this *"Yehi Ratzon"* is said every day, even by a *Kohen* or a *Levi* or one who can trace his genealogy to a particular tribe?

ANSWER: The uniqueness of a Jewish person is reflected in his *neshamah* — soul — which is truly a part of Hashem above (see *Tanya* ch. 2). Hashem sent down 600,000 souls to this world (ibid. ch. 37), and each one has a mission to accomplish. Until the soul completely accomplishes its task, sparks of the soul are reincarnated in newly born people.

Moreover, in addition to *gilgul* — transmigration — in which the soul is attached to a body and dominated by it, there is also *ibur neshamot* — impregnation of souls — in which a spark of the soul of a *tzaddik* is "impregnated" in another soul and serves as an additional spiritual charge for the soul of the recipient (see *Tanya* ch. 14).

Consequently, although the soul originated in a person who was a member of a particular tribe, it is possible that now this soul is in a person of another tribe, or has the soul of another person "impregnated" in it. Hence, this prayer, which is on behalf of the soul of the Jew, can be said by every individual, even a *Kohen* or *Levi*, or one who knows his tribal affiliation.

(לקוטי שיחות חל"ב ע' 21)

"ויהי המקריב ביום הראשון את קרבנו נחשון בן עמינדב ... וקרבנו..."

"The one who brought his offering on the first day was Nachshon son of Aminadav... and his offering...." (7:12-13)

QUESTION: Why is it written *"vekarbano"* — *"and* his offering" — regarding Nachshon ben Aminadav?

ANSWER: According to the *Midrash* (see Rashi 7:19), it was Netaneil ben Tzuar the *Nasi* of Yissachar who suggested that all the *nesi'im* bring offerings. Anyone who encourages others to do good deeds receives a reward for the encouragement and also shares the merit of the deeds themselves.

Therefore, although Nachshon ben Aminadav brought his offering first, it is written *"and* his offering" to indicate that the merit was not entirely his, but shared with Netanel.

(שער בת רבים)

* * *

Alternatively, to be the first to bring an offering was a great honor which might have made him conceited. The Torah wrote the extra "וי" — *"and* his offering" — to indicate that being first had no ill effect on him; on the contrary, he considered himself as someone who followed others.

(דעת זקנים מבעלי התוספות)

"ביום השני הקריב נתנאל בן צוער...הקריב את קרבנו"

"On the second day Nethaneil son of Tzuar offered ... he brought his offering." (7:18-19)

QUESTION: Why are the words *"hikriv et karbano"* — "he brought his offering" — said only for Netaneil ben Tzuar?

ANSWER: It was Netaneil ben Tzuar who suggested that all the *nesi'im* bring offerings. Since he was the one who proposed it, he shared in the merit of the offerings brought each day. However, on the second day, when Netaneil ben Tzuar brought his own offering, the Torah stresses that "he brought *his* offering" — he received full credit for the offering and the idea.

(כתב סופר)

"ביום השביעי נשיא לבני אפרים...."

"On the seventh day, the leader of the children of Ephraim..." (7:48)

QUESTION: Why did the leader of the tribe of Ephraim bring his offering on the seventh day — *Shabbat?*

ANSWER: When Yosef came to Egypt he was sold as a slave into the house of Potifar. The Torah relates that one day he came home to do his work, and Potifar's wife urged him to commit a transgression. Yosef became very frightened and ran away. According to the *Midrash (Yalkut Shimoni* 146), it was *Shabbat* and he came home to do "his work," which was to study and review the Torah his father taught him.

According to the *Gemara (Sanhedrin* 43b) when one resists and overpowers evil, it is equivalent to offering a sacrifice. Since Yosef "offered" a sacrifice on *Shabbat,* Hashem rewarded him that his descendent — the head of his son's tribe — would bring sacrifices for the dedication of the Altar on *Shabbat.*

(הדרש והעיון)

* * *

Alternatively, according to *Midrash Rabbah* (14:2), Yosef observed the *Shabbat* [in Egypt] before it was given as a *mitzvah* for the Jewish people to observe. This is inferred from the *pasuk,* "Have the meat slaughtered *vehachein* — and prepare it" (*Bereishit* 43:16). The word *"hachein"* is primarily used to express preparation for *Shabbat,* as may be inferred from the *pasuk*, "It shall be on that the sixth day, *veheichinu* — when they prepare" (*Shemot* 16:5). Hashem, therefore, said to him, "Yosef, you observed the *Shabbat* before the Torah was given; I promise I shall repay your grandson by allowing him to present his offering on *Shabbat*. Although an individual is otherwise forbidden to do so, I will accept his offering favorably."

Is it not puzzling that the reward for Yosef's *Shabbat* observance would be his son's desecration of the *Shabbat*?

Hashem gave us the *Shabbat* and commanded us to sanctify it. This is accomplished by refraining from all the forbidden labors, including bringing an offering. On the other hand, there are sacrifices which we are commanded to offer specifically on *Shabbat*. Obviously, an offering prescribed by Hashem is no *Shabbat* desecration, but a means to enhance the holiness of *Shabbat*.

Yosef's reward was that, inspite of the usually forbidden status of individual sacrifices offered on *Shabbat*, by Divine provision, his grandson's offering on *Shabbat* would not be treated as a usual individual sacrifice, but as a required *Shabbat* sacrifice through which the holiness of that *Shabbat* would be elevated and enhanced.

(לקוטי שיחות חכ"ג)

"כיום העשירי... נשיא לבני דן...."

"On the tenth day, the leader of the children of Dan...." (7:66)

QUESTION: Why was the tenth day of *Nissan* set aside for the tribe of Dan?

ANSWER: When Yaakov blessed his children, he associated the power of earthly judgment with the tribe of Dan saying, "Dan shall judge his people as one of the tribes of Israel" (*Bereishit* 49:16).

The tenth of *Nissan* always occurs on the same day of the week as the first day of *Rosh Hashanah*, when Hashem judges

His people. Therefore the prince of the tribe associated with earthly judgment brings his offering on a day which is associated with Divine judgment.

(אוצר חיים)

"זאת חנכת המזבח ביום המשח אתו מאת נשיאי ישראל
קערת כסף שתים עשרה מזרקי כסף שנים עשר כפות זהב שתים עשרה
כפות זהב שתים עשרה עשרה מלאת קטרת"

**"This was the dedication of the Altar on the
day it was anointed from the princes of Israel:
twelve silver bowls, twelve silver basins.
Twelve gold ladles, filled with incense."
(7:84, 86)**

QUESTION: Each *nasi* brought a gold ladle filled with incense and a silver bowl and basin, both filled with fine flour mixed with oil (7:13). Why does the verse giving the tallies of bowls, basins, and ladles state that the ladles were filled with incense while it omits that the bowls and basins were filled with flour and oil?

ANSWER: According to the *Midrash Rabbah* (12:21), all the *nesi'im* came to the *Mishkan* with their offerings on *Rosh Chodesh Nissan,* the first day of the dedication. Afterwards, they were told that *"nasi echad layom"* — *only* one *nasi* per day should present his offering.

When a meal-offering or incense is put into a holy utensil, it must be offered on that day. If it is left in the utensil overnight, it becomes disqualified for further use (see *Me'ilah* 9a, *Shavuot* 11a, *Tosafot*). If so, how was it possible for the *nesi'im* to bring the incense and flour mixed with oil on *Rosh Chodesh* and yet offer it on a subsequent day?

We can answer this question by citing two rules: 1) The different spices of the incense needed to be ground and then mixed together *within* the Sanctuary (Rambam, *K'lei Hamikdash* 2:6).

2) Only if the flour is together with the oil in the same utensil must it be offered immediately and not left overnight.

Hence, on *Rosh Chodesh* each *nasi* brought a gold ladle filled with unground and unmixed incense. Consequently, although it was in the ladle, it did not become disqualified by staying overnight. However, the flour and oil were not brought together in the bowl because they would become disqualified if not offered on the same day. Therefore, they were brought separately and only on the day which was designated for the *nasi* to bring his offering did he bring the flour mixed with oil for a meal-offering in the silver bowls and basins.

The tally in the Torah is for all the offerings which were brought on *Rosh Chodesh* "on the day it was anointed." On that day they all brought ladles containing *unground* incense, and silver bowls and basins which were *not* filled at that time with fine flour mixed with oil.

(פרדס יוסף החדש, ועי' כלי חמדה)

"זאת חנכת המזבח ביום המשח אתו...

זאת חנכת המזבח אחרי המשח אתו"

"This was the dedication of the Altar, on the day it was anointed...This was the dedication of the Altar after it was anointed." (7:84, 88)

QUESTION: Why does it say "*on* the day it was anointed" in the first *pasuk,* and four *pesukim* later it says "*after* it was anointed"?

ANSWER: It is common for people to cherish something new. As time passes, however, the novelty often proves short-lived. For example, a boy preparing for his *Bar Mitzvah* often begins putting on his *tefillin* with excitement and lofty intentions. As he grows older, unfortunately, it becomes a daily routine, and even while wearing his *tefillin* he gives them little attention.

On the day the Altar was anointed, everybody was in high spirits. The Torah is telling us that not only were they in great spirits "on the day the Altar was anointed," but that even *"after* it was anointed," it did not lose its newness, but was cherished with the same love and awe as on the first day.

(חידושי הרי"ם)

"בהעלתך את הנרת"
"When you kindle the lamps...." (8:2)

QUESTION: Rashi explains that the word *"beha'alotecha"* (literally "when you step up") is used because there was a *ma'aleh* — step — in front of the *Menorah* on which the *Kohen* stood as he prepared the wicks and oil of the *Menorah*.

The height of the *Menorah* was only three *amot*, approximately five feet; why did Aharon need to stand on a step in order to reach the top of the *Menorah*?

ANSWER: Aharon, as *Kohen Gadol*, wore the *tzitz* — forehead-plate — and according to *halachah* it was forbidden for the *Kohen Gadol* to raise his hands above it (Rambam, *Nesi'at Kapayim* 14:9). It was therefore necessary to have steps in front of the *Menorah* so that when the *Kohen Gadol* would kindle the lights he would be able to do so without lifting his hands above the permitted height.

(תפארת יהונתן)

"בהעלתך את הנרת"
"When you kindle the lamps...." (8:2)

QUESTION: Rashi writes that the word, *"beha'alotecha"* teaches us that there were steps in front of the *Menorah* upon which the *Kohen* would stand and prepare the candles. Why does Rashi in *Chumash Shemot* (27:20) explain that the word *"leha'a lot [neir tamid]"* — "to kindle [a light continuously]" — means, to kindle until the flame rises up by itself and does not say that *"leha'alot"* teaches us that there was a step?

ANSWER: In *Chumash Shemot*, Hashem instructs Moshe that the Jews should bring *him* oil in order to kindle the *Menorah*. When the *Mishkan* was erected, for the first seven days Moshe served as the *Kohen Gadol* and performed the service in the *Mishkan*. The *Gemara (Berachot* 54b) says that Moshe was ten *amot* tall (approximately 16 feet). Thus, when he kindled the *Menorah* he did not need any step to stand on, for he was much taller than the *Menorah*. Therefore, Rashi explains that the word *"leha'alot"* teaches us a rule about how to kindle the *Menorah* itself.

However, *Parshat Beha'alotecha* discusses the kindling of the *Menorah* by Aharon and his descendants throughout the generations. Since many *Kohanim* were not very tall and it is forbidden for a *Kohen Gadol* to raise his hands above the *tzitz* — forehead plate — Rashi writes that the *Kohen* would stand on a step while kindling the *Menorah*.

(פון אונזער אלטען אוצר)

"בהעלתך את הנרת אל מול פני המנורה יאירו שבעת הנרות"

**"When you will kindle the lamps,
towards the face of the *Menorah*
shall the seven lamps cast light." (8:2)**

QUESTION: Why is the word *"Haneirot"* (הנרת) — "the lamps" — first written without a י and then with a י (הנרות)?

ANSWER: The *Midrash (Bamidbar Rabbah* 15:5) says that the juxtaposition of the *parshah* dealing with the *Menorah* kindling and the dedication-offerings of the princes indicates that Aaron became disheartened when neither he nor his tribe participated with the princes of the tribes in the dedication. Therefore, Hashem said to Moshe: "Go and tell Aaron: Fear not! You are designated for something of greater importance than this. The offerings are brought only as long as the Sanctuary is in existence, but the lamps will *give light in front of the candelabrum* forever."

Now it is an obvious fact that when the Sanctuary is not in existence and the offerings are not brought because of its destruction, the lighting of the lamps of the *Menorah* in the Sanctuary also ceases, so what does the *Midrash* mean in saying that G-d promised Aaron that the lighting of the lamps would never stop?

The Ramban explains that the Sages of the *Midrash* are teaching that this Torah portion is alluding to the lights of the Dedication of the Hasmoneans, which applies on the festival of *Chanukah* even after the destruction of the Sanctuary, in our exile.

A popular question regarding *Chanukah* is raised by the *Beit Yosef* (*Tur Orach Chaim* 670): Since the flask of oil was sufficient to last for one day, so that the actual miracle was only for seven days, why do we celebrate eight days? Among the many answers to this question are the following two:

1) Concerned that they would not have oil for the subsequent days, they divided the flask into eight portions. Every day they would only fill the *Menorah* with 1/8 of the usual amount of oil and miraculously the *Menorah* remained burning the entire night.

(בית יוסף סי׳ עת״ר)

2) They thinned down the wicks to 1/8 of their normal thickness. Thus, only 1/8 of the normal amount of oil would be needed for the entire night. Though the light of the *Menorah* would now be very dim, they thought it would be better to have a dim light for eight days than to have the regular light for one day and miss kindling the *Menorah* the other seven days. Miraculously, the very thin wicks produced the same beautiful flame as the usual ones did.

(פנים יפות)

Perhaps our *pasuk* is hinting to these two explanations: "[A time will come] when you will kindle the *neirot* [without a ו - הנרת] — and they will be lacking in fullness, either because you will not have a sufficient amount of oil or due to the thinness of the wicks; nevertheless, I will perform a miracle and *Ya'iru shivat haneirot* [with a ו - הנרות] — the seven lamps will cast a full light — they will burn the entire night regardless of the reduced amount of oil or the light will be completely bright regardless of the thinned down wicks."

(נרות שמונה)

"אל מול פני המנורה יאירו שבעת הנרות"

"Toward the face of the *Menorah* shall the seven lamps cast light." (8:2)

QUESTION: There is a "wondrous *Midrash*" that states in connection to this *pasuk* "Peitach devarecha ya'ir" — "Your opening words illuminate" (Psalms 119:130).

What is the meaning of this *Midrash*?

ANSWER: The *Menorah* had seven branches, nine flowers, eleven knobs, and twenty-two cups, and according to the *Gemara* (Menachot 28b) it was eighteen *tefachim* (handbreadths) tall.

The *Midrash* by quoting the *pasuk* "your opening words illuminate" is alluding that the "opening words," i.e. the first *pasuk* of each of the five *chumashim*, have a connection to a part of the *Menorah*.

The first *pasuk* of *Bereishit* contains seven words, corresponding to the seven branches of the *Menorah*. The first *pasuk* of *Shemot* contains eleven words, which correspond to the eleven knobs of the *Menorah*. The first *pasuk* of *Vayikra* has nine words, corresponding to the nine flowers. The first *pasuk* of *Bamidbar* has seventeen words, and counting the entire *pasuk* as one (known in *gematria* as "im hakolel"), corresponds to the height of the *Menorah*. The first *pasuk* of *Devarim* has twenty-two words for the twenty-two cups of the *Menorah*.

(אדרת אליהו והגהות הגר"י בכרך פסחים ו' ע"ב)

Alternatively, though the *Gemara* (Menachot 28b) says that the *Menorah* was eighteen *tefachim* tall, it was actually only somewhat over seventeen. Thus the first *pasuk* of *Bamidbar* has one word for each full *tefach* of the *Menorah*'s height.

(תורת העולה להרמ"א ח"א פט"ז, ילקוט ראובני תרומה בשם כוונת אר"י)

"ויעש כן אהרן אל מול פני המנורה העלה נרתיה כאשר צוה ה' את משה"

"Aaron did so; toward the face of the *Menorah* he kindled its lamps, as Hashem had commanded Moshe." (8:3)

QUESTION: The word *"kein"* — "so" — is superfluous?

ANSWER: Why, on the first day of creation when Hashem made light, does the Torah omit the phrase *"vayehi chein"* — "and it was so" — as it says in regard to many of the other items of the six days of creation?

The *Gemara* (*Chagigah* 12a) says that originally Hashem gave the world an extremely powerful light. Afterwards, He saw that it was not fitting that the wicked use it, so He set it aside for the righteous to be used by them in the future. Therefore, since the light that continued to serve the world was not the original one created, the words *"vayehi chein"* — "and it was so" — are omitted.

When Aharon would light the *Menorah*, it was not an ordinary physical kindling for illumination purposes. Rather, he would bring into the Sanctuary a reflection of the *ohr haganuz* — light which was hidden — for the righteous. With the extra word *"kein"* the Torah is alluding to Aharon's accomplishment when he kindled the *Menorah*: that the original light of creation (which was alluded to at creation by the omitted word *"kein"*) should be in this world.

(חנוכת התורה)

"ויעש כן אהרן אל מול פני המנורה העלה נרתיה כאשר צוה ה' את משה"

"And Aharon did so; toward the face of the *Menorah* he kindled its lamps, as G-d had commanded Moshe." (8:3)

QUESTION: Rashi explains that the Torah emphasizes that "Aharon did so" to declare Aharon's praise — *"shelo shinah"* — that he did not act differently.

Would anyone suspect that Aharon would deviate from Hashem's command?

ANSWER: Aharon, as *Kohen Gadol,* kindled the *Menorah* the entire 40 years that the *Mishkan* was in the wilderness. A person naturally does something the first time with more dedication and excitement than after he has done it for several years. In his praise, the Torah says that Aharon did not change: Even after kindling the *Menorah* for many years, he continued to do so with the same dedication, fervor, and excitement as the first time.

(לקוטי בתר לקוטי)

Alternatively, Aharon was an *"oheiv shalom verodeif shalom"* — "lover of peace and pursuer of peace" (*Pirkei Avot* 1:12) — and was therefore loved by every Jew. An ordinary citizen is often affable and involved with people and their needs. However, a person who is appointed to a high office may become conceited and distant.

Aharon's greatness is that even when he became *Kohen Gadol,* holding the second highest position in the Jewish community, *"lo shinah"* — he did not change toward his fellow man — he still remained the same *"oheiv shalom verodeif shalom"* — "lover and pursuer of peace."

(ר' מאיר זצ"ל מפרעמישלאן)

"אם בדרכי תלך ואם את משמרתי תשמר...
ונתתי לך מהלכים בין העומדים האלה"

"If you will walk in My ways and safeguard My charge... I will permit Your movement among these immobile [angels]." (*Haftarat Shabbat Chanukah*)

QUESTION: What is the significance of this blessing?

ANSWER: A soul descends to this world to accomplish in Torah and *Mitzvot.* With every *mitzvah* performed, the soul and the person are continuously elevated. During one's lifetime, man is a *mehalech* — one who "goes," i.e. constantly progresses. He keeps going from one level to a higher level of holiness. When man expires he ceases being a *mehalech* — and becomes an *omeid* — stationary — he no longer can do *mitzvot* and thus the continuous ascent generated by his *mitzvot* performance comes to a halt. However, if one has children who walk in the path of Torah, the parents can earn merit through their good deeds and thus in their heavenly abode they continue to be *mehalchim* — ones who ascend to higher levels in their children's merit.

Hashem is promising Joshua the *Kohen Gadol* "If you will walk in My ways and safeguard My watch, you will then merit to have children who observe Torah and *mitzvot,* and thus through them, you will progress even when you will no longer be a *mehalech* on this world and be among the *omdim* — those who can no longer can do *mitzvot* which would earn them continuous elevation. I will grant you children who are *mehalchin* — ones who walk in the path of Torah — and through them you will continue your spiritual ascent even when you are among the *omdin.*"

(חתם סופר)

*   *   *

There is a popular saying *"B'ra kare'eih d'avuha"* — "A son is the leg of the father. This means that he is an extension of the father. But why compare him to the leg and not to the hand or mouth etc. of the father?

In light of the above it could mean the following: A person's mobility is through his legs. With the legs one walks and through them one can reach considerable heights. Once the father dies he becomes immobile and can no longer attain new heights.

However, if the father has sons who live in accordance with Torah and *mitzvot,* they now become his "legs," and in merit of their good deeds he continues to go on to new heights in his heavenly abode.

ימי חנוכה
Days of Chanukah

FIFTH DAY OF *CHANUKAH*
ZOT *CHANUKAH*
MY *ZEIDE'S CHANUKAH* MESSAGE

ה' חנוכה

"ה' חנוכה"

"Fifth Day of *Chanukah*"

QUESTION: What is the uniqueness of the fifth day of *Chanukah*?

ANSWER: The fifth day of *Chanukah* can never occur on a *Shabbat*. When *Chanukah* occurs on days that are even only *potentially Shabbat* days, the light of *Chanukah* combines with the light of *Shabbat* for a powerful illumination. So the fifth night, which can *never* be *Shabbat*, represents great darkness relative to the other nights. Thus, the fifth light of *Chanukah* has the unique task and power to illuminate and instill spirituality even in such a time of darkness.

Similarly, it is the duty of every Jew, wherever he may find himself, be it in Warsaw, England, the United States or Canada, to illuminate even the heaviest darkness.

(כפר חב"ד גליון 624 ע' 23 בשם כ"ק אדמו"ר - ווארשא תרפ"ט)

In *Chabad* circles this day is of special significance because the *Alter* Rebbe, Rabbi Shneur Zalman of Liadi, the founder of Chabad *Chassidut*, was released from his second imprisonment on the fifth day of *Chanukah*, in the year תקס"א — 5561.

He was imprisoned because the government scholars thought that some of the topics accentuated and expanded in his *Chassidic* philosophy might cause insubordination to the government and refusal to engage in practical matters, which are necessary for the existence of the state. Upon articulately clarifying his teaching and dispelling their fears, he gained his release.

(סיפורי חסידים-מועדים)

"ה' חנוכה"

"Fifth Day of *Chanukah*"

QUESTION: In the *Gemara* (*Shabbat* 21b) *Beit Shammai* is of the opinion that on the first night of *Chanukah* one should light eight candles and decrease the number by one each night. *Beit Hillel,* has an opposite view. On the first night light one candle and each succeeding night increase it by one.

How does their distinctive personal character effect their view as to how many candles one should light each night of *Chanukah,* and what significance does their views have on the fifth day of *Chanukah?*

ANSWER: The views and opinions one expresses are a product of his character and nature; e.g. an intrinsically good-natured and congenial person sees things in a positive and favorable light, while a harsh person who is stern and austere will commonly take a negative and pessimistic approach. Hence, the *halachah* differences of *Beit Shammai* and *Beit Hillel* are an expression of their respective character traits.

Shammai and Hillel were of opposing natures, and their views in Torah reflect their mental dispositions, which they transmitted to their students — *Beit Shammai* — the school of Shammai and *Beit Hillel* — the school of Hillel.

The *Gemara* (*Shabbat* 30b) says that Hillel was very humble and gentle. Shammai, on the other hand, was stern and unyielding. It was not difficult to provoke Shammai and cause him to lose his temper, but Hillel was extremely patient and would never take offense. For example, when a prospective proselyte once came to Shammai asking to be converted and making preposterous requests, Shammai became exasperated and pushed him away, while Hillel accepted him cordially and warmly.

The significance of lighting *Chanukah* candles on the outside, when it is dark, is that the "street" which is dark — alien to Torah and sometimes even actively hostile to Torah — must be illuminated and be converted into a "friendly domain" and become an ally to the authentic Torah philosophy.

The Sages of *Shammai* and *Hillel* have diverse opinions as to how this is accomplished, based on the two different approaches to serving Hashem. One approach is *"Sur mei'ra"* — "Turn away from — i.e. abandon" — evil, and the other is

"Asei tov" — "Do good." The philosophy of *"Sur mei'ra"* is to vehemently fight evil until it is eradicated. The policy of *"Asei tov"* is to accentuate and intensify the doing of good until the evil is overpowered and eventually dissipates by itself.

Beit Shammai favors the *"Sur mei'ra"* approach. This is comparable to strategy in a war: the initial attack has to be fierce and overwhelming, and once the enemy is destroyed, all that is necessary is to clean up the remnants. Similarly, with the *"Sur mei'ra"* approach the first attack must be devastating, and then once the enemy is shattered minor attacks follow till it is totally conquered. Therefore, they hold that to properly eradicate the enemy — the roaming forces that are alien to Torah and *Yiddishkeit* — at the outset a strong pillar of light is needed — eight candles. Once a breakthrough is made, the rest of the battle can be accomplished with less weaponry.

Beit Hillel, favors the *"Asei tov"* approach. Cognizant that a little bit of light dispels much darkness, they hold that one should always accentuate the good and add in one's activities little by little. Eventually, the antagonists will be so affected by the illumination that they will convert and totally join your forces.

The fifth night of *Chanukah* has a special significance in demonstrating the prevalence of the *"Asei tov"* approach over the *Sur mei'ra"* approach. This is the first night when following the approach of *Beit Hillel* results in more illumination on the *Menorah,* since we light five candles according to *Beit Hillel* and only four candles according to *Beit Shammai.* It is thus on this night that the approach of ever-increasing illumination overtakes the approach of constant decrease and the progression towards maximum illumination begins to prevail.

The study of *Chassidut* emphasizes the *"Asei tov"* approach, unlike *Mussar* — study of ethics — which follows the *"Sur mei'ra"* philosophy. Therefore, in Chassidic circles, the fifth night of *Chanukah* is considered an auspicious time.

(עי׳ לקו״ש חכ״ה ע׳ 396)

זאת חנוכה

"זאת חנוכה"
"Zot Chanukah — This is Chanukah."

QUESTION: Why is the eighth day of *Chanukah* called *"Zot Chanukah"*?

ANSWER: The construction of the *Mishkan* — Tabernacle — which the Jews built in the wilderness was completed on the 25th of *Kislev*. However, it was not officially dedicated until *Rosh Chodesh Nissan*, the month in which the Patriarchs were born (*Rosh Hashanah* 11a). Hashem paid back the month of *Kislev* with the rededication of the *Beit Hamikdash* through the Hasmoneans on the 25th of *Kislev*.

For the dedication of the *Mishkan*, on every day of the first twelve days of the month a *Nasi* — prince of a tribe — brought a battery of offerings. Thus, it is customary to read on each day of *Chanukah* a Biblical portion which describes the offering of one of the *Nessi'im* (*Bamidbar* 7:1-8:4). The Torah reading on the eighth day starts with the offering of the *Nasi* of the tribe of Menasheh and goes through all the other *Nessi'im*. Basically every offering was the same and the language of the portion is identical except for the change of name. This is followed by a tally of all the items brought by all the *Nessi'im* together, which is also read on the eighth day. Since it starts with the word *"Zot chanukat hamizbei'ach"* — "This was the dedication of the Altar" (7:74), the eighth day is named *"Zot Chanukah."*

* * *

Alternatively, there is a popular question asked by the *Beit Yosef* that *Chanukah* should only be celebrated seven days since they found a single flask of oil which was sufficient for one day, and thus, the miraculous kindling was only for seven days? One of the answers is that *Chanukah* is really only seven days and the holiday lasts eight days because of *sefeika deyoma*

— a doubt as to which day was declared as *Rosh Chodesh* and thus a lack of clarity as to which day of the month is really the 25th of *Kislev* (see p. 42).

Most commentaries do not accept this theory, and therefore the eighth day is called *"Zot Chanukah"* — *"This* is *Chanukah"* — to emphasize that it is an actual day of the eight-day celebration and not merely a day celebrated due to ambiguity in the calendar.

(עיטורי תורה בשם לחם אשר)

"זאת חנוכה"

"Zot Chanukah — This is Chanukah."

QUESTION: How did the name *Zot Chanukah* for the eighth day originate?

ANSWER: One of the answers of the *Beit Yosef's* question that *Chanukah* should be celebrated only seven days since they had oil for one day, is that the Syrian-Greeks intended to abolish *Shabbat* observance, *Rosh Chodesh* and *Brit Milah* — circumcision. Therefore an eight-day festival was declared because in the eight day period starting with the 25th of *Kislev* there is always at least one *Shabbat*, at least one day of *Rosh Chodesh* (*Tevet*), and a possibility of a circumcision on the eighth day. Therefore, in order to commemorate their failure to abolish circumcision, we have the eighth day of *Chanukah*.

When Hashem commanded Avraham concerning circumcision, He said *"zot beriti"* — "this is my covenant [which you shall keep between Me and your descendants after you. Every male should be circumcised" — *Bereishit* 17:10]. Since the eighth day of *Chanukah* is celebrated because of *Brit Milah,* which is called *"zot"* — the day is called *zot Chanukah.*

"זאת חנוכה"

"Zot Chanukah — This is Chanukah."

QUESTION: What is the uniqueness of the eighth day over the previous seven days of *Chanukah*?

ANSWER: The significance of the number eight is that it transcends the realm of this mundane and physical world and alludes to the exalted and holy. In the natural world, time is based on a seven-day week and all occurrences are controlled by *sheva kochavei lechet* — the *seven* orbital planets. Hashem transcends all this, and therefore the number eight represents His lofty Holiness.

In the era of *Mashiach* we will merit a higher revelation of G-dliness, and therefore *Mashiach's* harp will consist of eight strings, one more than the seven-stringed harp of the *Beit Hamikdash* (*Arachin* 13b).

Chanukah is a preparation for the forthcoming Messianic era. These days are called *"Chanukah"* because they are a *Chinuch* — education/preparation — accustoming us to the final redemption. During the candle lighting we are treated to a resemblance of the illumination of the *Or Haganuz* — hidden primordial light — which will radiate in full glory in the days of *Mashiach*.

The candles and light of *Chanukah* are analogous to Torah and *mitzvot* as King Shlomo said, "For a *mitzvah* is a candle and Torah is light" (Proverbs 6:23). During *Chanukah* an increase in Torah study is preferred since through the *Ohr Chadash* — new light of Torah that we add in the world we will accomplish the purpose of creation and merit the revelation of the new light which transcends our mundane world — the light of *Mashiach*.

The correlation of *Chanukah* and *Mashiach* is most evident on day eight, because the number eight represents that which is above the chain of creation (סדר השתלשלות). Similarly, the Messianic era will usher in a new order which will also transcend the chain of creation.

(התוועדיות תשמ"ח ח"ב ע' 119)

"זאת חנוכה... ביום השמיני נשיא לבני מנשה"

"Zot Chanukah — This is Chanukah."
"On the eighth day the prince
for the tribe of Menasheh." (Bamidbar 7:54)

QUESTION: What is the connection between the name *"Zot Chanukah"* for the eighth day of *Chanukah* and the Torah reading of the *Nasi* of Menasheh on the eighth day?

ANSWER: The Torah relates that when Yosef brought his sons Ephraim and Menasheh to be blessed by Yaakov, he placed Ephraim with his right [hand] to Yaakovs left, and Menasheh with his left to Yaakov's right [hand]. Yaakov maneuvered his hands so that his right hand would be on Ephraim and his left on Menasheh. This displeased Yosef and he tried to remove Yaakov's right hand from upon Ephraim and place it on Menasheh since he was the firstborn. Yaakov refused, saying "I know my son I know, he too will become a people and he too will become great; however, his younger brother shall become greater than he." He then blessed them, saying "By you Israel shall bless, saying, 'May Hashem make you like Ephraim and Menasheh' and he put Ephraim before Menasheh" (*Bereishit* 48:9-20).

What is the philosophical reason for their different opinion who should receive priority? King David says *"Sur mei'ra va'asei tov"* — "Abandon evil and do good" (Psalms 34:15). King David's two admonitions are actually two separate ways in man's service of Hashem, and there is a question which of the two should be primary.

Yosef was of the opinion that first and foremost one should rid himself of any relation with evil and only afterward should he work on *"Asei tov"* — doing good. This is evident from the names he gave his two sons: Menasheh and Ephraim. As the Torah relates, "The firstborn he called Menasheh because Hashem has made me forget all my hardship and all my father's household." And the name of the second son he called Ephraim for, 'Hashem made me fruitful in the land of my suffering'" (*Bereishit* 41:51-52).

That is, first he thanked Hashem for helping to achieve his endeavor of *Sur mei'ra* — ridding himself of any negativity and grievance toward his family or the toil and difficulties he endured in Egypt. Then he thanked Hashem for helping him to accomplish his second endeavor of *Asei tov* — becoming fruitful with positive achievements in the land of his suffering.

On the other hand, Yaakov was of the opinion that while this may be a proper order of service for a *Tzaddik* like Yosef, ordinary people should accentuate the *Asei tov* — doing good — approach because "a small amount of light dispels much darkness" (*Tanya* ch. 12). Hence, he gave preference to what Ephraim represents and said that *Klal Yisrael* in general, should give primacy to the service of Hashem represented by Ephraim.

In regard to how the *mehadrin* — scrupulous — should conduct themselves with *Chanukah* candle lighting, there is a dispute between *Beit Shammai* and *Beit Hillel*. *Beit Shammai* says to light eight on the first night and to light one less each succeeding night until on the eighth night only one candle is lit. *Beit Hillel* opines the reverse, instructing to start with one candle on the on first night and add one more each succeeding night, so that on the eighth night eight candles are lit.

It can be explained that their disputes also hinge on the question as to which approach should be given primacy, *Sur mei'ra* or *Asei tov*. *Beit Shammai* prefers the *Sur mei'ra* approach and *Beit Hillel* favors the *Asei tov* approach.

A significance of lighting *Chanukah* candles on the outside, when it is dark, is that the "street" which is dark — alien to Torah and sometimes even actively hostile to Torah — must be illuminated and be converted into a "friendly domain" and become an ally to the authentic Torah philosophy.

With the *"Sur mei'ra"* approach the first attack must be devastating, and then, once the enemy is shattered minor attacks follow until it is totally conquered. Therefore, they hold that to properly eradicate the enemy — the roaming forces that are alien to Torah and *Yiddishkeit* — at the outset a strong pillar of light is needed — eight candles. Once a breakthrough is made the rest of the battle can be accomplished with less.

Beit Hillel, favors the *"Asei tov"* approach. Cognizant that a little bit of light dispels much darkness, they hold that one should always accentuate the good and add in one's activities little by little. Eventually, the antagonists will be so affected by the illumination that they will convert and totally join the forces of light. (See p. 179 for an elaboration on this.)

Thus, *Beit Shammai* follow Yosef's theory which gives preference to Menasheh over Ephraim, and *Beit Hillel* follows Yaakov's theory which gives priority to Ephraim.

Since on the seventh day of *Chanukah* we read about the offering made by the prince of Ephraim and on the eighth we read about the offering of the prince of Menasheh, obviously, Yaakov's approach of putting Ephraim before Menasheh is the prevailing one.

One of the explanations given to the name *"Chanukah"* is that it is an acronym for *"Chet neirot v'halachah kebeit Hillel"* (ח׳ נרות והלכה כבית הלל) — "Light eight candles and the *halachah* is according to *Beit Hillel*" — that each night you add one more candle. Thus, from *Chanukah* we can learn that the *Asei tov* approach should be accentuated over the *Sur mei'ra* approach.

Hence, on the eighth day when we read about Menasheh *after* having read of Ephraim the day before, and we light the complete total of eight candles, we call the day *"Zot Chanukah"* — *"this* is Chanukah" — because on this day we demonstrate what *Chanukah* is all about.

Chanukah's message is that the preferred way to succeed in illuminating the world is the *Asei tov* approach. With kindness, goodness and *ahavat Yisrael* we will more easily achieve Hashem's purpose of creation — to make this mundane world a dwelling place for the Holy One, blessed be He.

(עי׳ לקוטי שיחות חכ״ה ע׳ 396, ועיטורי תורה פ׳ ויחי)

My Zeide's *Chanukah* Message*

Parshat Mikeitz is always read during *Chanukah*. In it we read about Yosef's rise to glory in the land of Egypt and we also learn about his marriage and family. The Torah relates that "Yosef called the name of the firstborn Menasheh: for G-d has made me forget all my toil and my entire father's house. The second one he called Ephraim: for G-d has made me fruitful in the land of my suffering" (*Bereishit* 41:51-52).

Now we can easily understand the reasoning for naming a son "Ephraim." But that the righteous Yosef should express happiness and gratefulness for forgetting his father's house is very puzzling. Why would Yosef be happy and content for forgetting the home of Yaakov and its spiritual ambiance?

A visitor once entered a presumably kosher restaurant. Unimpressed with the religiosity of the personnel, he began to inquire about the *kashrut* standards. The proprietor confidently pointed to a picture on the wall of a Jew with a long beard and *peiyot*. He said to the visitor: "You see that man up there? He was my father!" The visitor replied: "If you were hanging on the wall, and your father was behind the counter, I would not ask any questions. But since your father is hanging on the wall, and you are behind the counter, I have good reason to question the *kashrut*."

There are many whose only attachment to *Yiddishkeit* is through nostalgia. They remember their mother's lighting candles, they recall the long beards and *peiyot* of their fathers, and they reminisce about their parents' *Shabbat* table. They proudly tell their children about it, but unfortunately they do not emulate or practice this way of life themselves.

Living among the Egyptians, Yosef was in danger of becoming totally assimilated in the society of the upper class. Fortunately, he remained tenacious in his Torah observance.

---

* For many years it was a custom in our family, to have a *Chanukah* party. The highlight was the message my grandfather, Rabbi Tzvi *Hakohen* ז"ע Kaplan would deliver. The following is the essence of some thoughts he expressed at these occasions.

Thus, it was unnecessary for him to tell his children about his parents' observance. He conducted his home exactly the same way as his father had done and was able to "forget" his father's house. When Yosef spoke to his children about Torah and *Yiddishkeit*, he did not have to suffice with reminiscing nostalgically about what went on in his father's house. Rather he was able to show his family his own home as a living example. It was a place where Torah study is in full vibrancy and *mitzvot* are a daily way of life.

* * *

In *Pirkei Avot* (6:8), Rabbi Shimon ben Yehudah states in the name of Rabbi Shimon ben Yochai that "children are something which is pleasing for the righteous and pleasing for the world." He supports this with proof from what King Shlomo said *"Ateret zekeinim b'nei banim, v'tiferet banim avotam"* — "Grandchildren are the crown of the aged, and the glory of children are their fathers" (Proverbs 17:6).

To prove that *"banim"* — "children" — are pleasing for the righteous it is sufficient to just state the first part of the *pasuk*, "Grandchildren are the crown of the aged." Why is it necessary to also quote the conclusion of the *pasuk*, "the glory of children are their fathers"?

Not always are the grandchildren the crown of the aged. Unfortunately, there are grandparents who are very disappointed with their grandchildren's alienation from Torah and *mitzvot*. For instance, how sad is it to grandparents when they know that they cannot eat at their grandchild's home because it is not kosher.

Thus, the *Beraita* is teaching that when *"tiferet banim avotom"* — "the glory of children are their fathers" — i.e. they are proud of their fathers who are strictly observant Jews and all their endeavors are to emulate them. Only then is it that *"ateret zekeinim b'nei banim"* — "grandchildren are the crown of the aged." To the grandparents who merited living to see this *nachas*, the grandchildren are a crown which they love and cherish immensely.

דינים
Dinim

MENORAH LIGHTING —
HOME,
SYNAGOGUE,
OUTDOORS
V'AL HANISSIM

It is customary to use oil lamps with cotton wicks for the *Menorah*. If unavailable, use paraffin candles in amounts large enough to burn until ½ hour after nightfall. A beeswax candle is used for the *shamash* (the candle used to kindle the lights).

(ספר המנהגים חב"ד, מנהג ישראל תורה, תרע"ג ה')

It is the *Chabad* custom to place the *Menorah* on a chair, or the like, within the doorway; next to the doorpost opposite the *mezuzah*. The *Menorah* should be three handbreadths above the floor and preferably lower than 10 handbreadths.

(תרע"א ר', ספר המנהגים חב"ד, כף החיים אות מ"ו

ואם צריך שגם הלהב יהי' בפחות מי' עי' מנהג ישראל תורה תרע"א ג' ונטעי גבריאל)

When kindling the *Menorah* in a room without a *mezuzah*, e.g. motel, the *Menorah* should be placed on the right side of the doorpost.

(סי' תרע"א, סעי' ז')

Those who place the *Menorah* on a windowsill facing the street should use a *Menorah* without a backsplash in order not to block the view of the lights from the household members or people on the street.

(שערי הלכה ומנהג ח"ב ע' ער"ד)

It is the *Chabad* custom to kindle the *Chanukah* lights after sunset, but before the appearance of the stars. If that is not possible, the lights should be kindled soon thereafter. Others light only after nightfall.

(סי' תרע"ב א', ועי' מ"ב וביאור הלכה)

If one did not kindle the *Chanukah* lights immediately after sunset, he may light them throughout the night with a *berachah*, providing some members of his household are awake. If it is after midnight and no members of his household are awake, one should nevertheless kindle but reciting a *berachah* is questionable.

(סי' תרע"ב מ"א סק"ו, ובאר היטב ושער הציון, אג"מ ח"ד או"ח סי' ק"ה ונטעי גבריאל)

The lights must burn for at least half an hour after nightfall. Before kindling the lights, one should make sure that there is enough oil (or if candles are used, that they are large

enough) to last at least 50 minutes. If they are kindled after
nightfall, it is sufficient that they burn for half an hour.

(פרמ״ג סתרע״ב א״א סק״ג, ועי׳ שו״ת ארץ צבי סי׳ קכ״א)

With the exception of Friday night, one should stay near
the *Chanukah* lights for approximately half an hour after
kindling them and study some Torah.

(שערי הלכה ומנהג ע׳ רע״ז, מנהג ישראל תורה תרע״ב ד׳ בשם מקור חיים)

If one of the lights goes out within this time, it is
customary to rekindle it.

(עי׳ נטעי גבריאל פל״ז סעי׳ ד׳ ובהנסמן שם)

No use should be made of the light shed by the *Chanukah*
lights, such as reading or working by their light.

(שם פל״ז)

It is customary for women not to work during the time the
Chanukah lights are required to burn.

(שו״ע סי׳ עת״ר סעי׳ א׳ ועי׳ נטעי גבריאל פל״ח מה נחשב מלאכה)

On the Friday of *Chanukah*, the *Chabad* custom is to recite
Minchah early. The *Chanukah* lights are then kindled (followed
by the *Shabbat* candles). Additional oil (or larger candles)
should be provided for these *Chanukah* lights, to make sure
they would last until half an hour after nightfall. Others recite
Minchah after lighting the *Menorah*.

(ספר המנהגים חב״ד, ועי׳ נטעי גבריאל פמ״ד סעי׳ ה׳. עי׳ סי׳ תרע״א סעי׳ ד׳ איך להתנהג בביהכנ״ס)

On Saturday night, *Maariv* should be prayed as soon as
possible, so that the *Menorah* can be kindled at the earliest
opportunity. The *Menorah* is kindled before *Havdalah* in the
synagogue, and at home after *Havdalah*.

(סי׳ תרפ״א סעי׳ ב׳ ובמ״ב וביה״ל)

The *Chanukah* lights must also be kindled in the
synagogue, but these do not absolve one from kindling the
Chanukah lights at home (not even the one who kindles them
in the synagogue).

(סי׳ תרע״א סעי׳ ז׳)

In the synagogue, the *Menorah* is placed on the southern
wall, and the lights are kindled between *Minchah* and *Maariv*.
The *Chabad* custom is that the *chazzan* stands with his back to

the north. Thus, on the first night, the candle on the west is lit first. In most synagogues, the *chazzan* stands with his back to the south, thus, on the first night, the easternmost candle is lit first.

(סי' תרע"א, כף החיים ס"ק ס"ט, ומ"ב ס"ק מ"ג)

On the first night, the *chazzan* recites the three blessings and kindles the candles. It is appropriate that there be ten men in the synagogue when the *Menorah* is kindled. The chazzan must also kindle a *Menorah* at home. If he lives alone, he does not recite the blessing *Shehechiyanu* when lighting the *Menorah* at home.

(סי' תרע"א סעי' ז' ובשערי תשובה ועי' נטעי גבריאל פמ"ג אודות ברכת שעשה נסים)

Before the morning service, the *Menorah* is rekindled in the synagogue, but the blessings are not recited.

(פמ"ג סי' עת"ר א"א סק"ב ועי' נטעי גבריאל פ"מ סעי' י"ח)

Kindling *Menorah* at public outdoor gatherings is a maximum *pirsumei nisa* and may be done with a *berachah*. However, all present should be urged not to rely on it for fulfillment of the *mitzvah,* and kindle in their homes.

(אז נדברו ח"ה סי' ל"ז וח"ו סע"ה)

A mourner during the eleven months of mourning following the death of a parent should continue to lead the communal prayers on *Chanukah.* However, he should not lead the *Hallel.*

(ספר המנהגים חב"ד נטעי גבריאל פנ"ה)

An announcement regarding the need to insert *V'al Hanissim* should be made before the evening service begins and not before the *Amidah.* One who forgot to make this addition, but realized the error before reciting G-d's name in the blessing ...הטוב שמך, should recite *V'al Hanissim* and conclude the blessing again. If G-d's name had already been mentioned, one should conclude the *Amidah* without adding *V'al Hanissim.*

(צ"צ שער המילואים או"ח סי' י"א)

One who recites the *Amidah* slowly should not intentionally skip *V'al Hanissim* in order to be able to respond to *Kedushah* or *Modim* with the congregation.

"ורשה קנים יצאים מצדיה שלשה קני מנרה מצדה האחד
ושלשה קני מנרה מצדה השני"

"And six branches going out of its sides; three branches of the *Menorah* out of its one side, and three branches of the *Menorah* out of its other side." (*Shemot* 25:32)

QUESTION: In what position were the branches and cups?

ANSWER: The Rambam wrote a commentary on *mishnayot* in Arabic which was recently newly translated to Hebrew in the Kapach Edition. This newer, more precise translation includes the Rambam's own drawing of the *Menorah* (*Menachot* 3:7). Evidently, the branches (*kanim*) of the *Menorah* were not curved like semi-circles, but instead were straight and extended diagonally upwards. (Rashi too is of this opinion.) The cups (*gevi'im*) were on the branches for beauty and were inverted with the wide end downward.

* * *

The popular image of the *Menorah* with curved branches stems from the *Menorah* which is engraved on the Arch of Titus in Rome. Titus was the Roman general who conquered Jerusalem and destroyed the second *Beit Hamikdash*. It was customary in those days to build a special gate through which the victorious soldiers would enter upon returning to their homeland.

On the Arch are engraved various scenes to commemorate the victory, and included is the *Menorah* which he defiled. The craftsmen made the *Menorah* according to a general idea of how it looked. However, according to the Rambam the *Menorah* on the Arch is an inaccurate replica of the one in the *Beit Hamikdash*.

(לקוטי שיחות חכ"א)

* * *

Some sources state that the cups were put with the wide end upwards in order to catch any dripping oil.

(חזקוני)

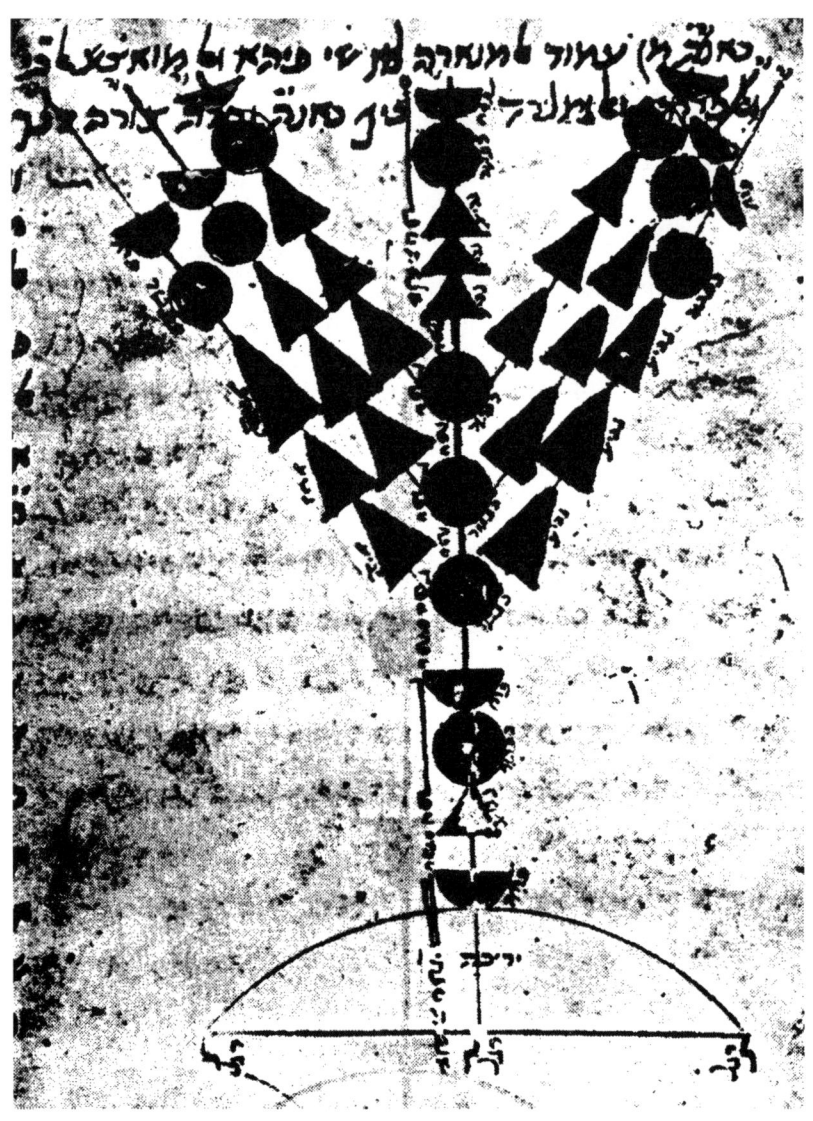

Facsimile of Rambam's own sketch of the *Menorah* in the *Beit Hamikdash*

"יערך אתו אהרן מערב עד בקר לפני ה'"

**"Aaron shall arrange it, from evening to
morning, before Hashem."** (*Vayikra* 24:3)

QUESTION: The *Menorah* was on the south side of the
Beit Hamikdash, how were the lamps positioned?

ANSWER: The *Beit Hamikdash* was rectangular, and the
entrance to it was in the east. The *Kodesh Hakadashim* — Holy
of Holies, i.e. innermost Sanctuary, was on the west. The
Menorah stood in the section known as "Holy." Now, there is
a dispute in *Gemara* (*Menachot* 98b) concerning the placement
of the *Menorah*. According to Rebbe the *Menorah* was placed in
the length of the *Beit Hamikdash*, i.e. the lamps were from east
to west. According to this opinion it was perpendicular to the
Parochet — partition — between the *Kodesh* — Holy — and
Kodesh Hakadashim — Holy of Holies. Rabbi Elazer ben Rabbi
Shimon opines that it stood in the width of the *Beit
Hamikdash;* i.e. the lamps were from north to south. Thus, it
was parallel to the *Parochet* which was on the west.

"להעלות נר תמיד מחוץ לפרוכת העדות ...
יערך אותו אהרן מערב עד בקר לפני ה' תמיד"

**"To kindle a lamp continually. Outside of the
Parochet of Testimony ... Aaron shall arrange it,
from evening to morning before Hashem
continually." (24:2,3)**

QUESTION: There were seven candles on the *Menorah*, so
why does it say *neir* — candle and *oto* — it — in singular?

ANSWER: The *Gemara* (*Shabbat* 22b) says that this *pasuk*
is referring to the *neir ma'aravi* — the western lamp — of the
Menorah. It served as a testimony for all mankind that the
Divine Presence dwells among the Jewish people.

The uniqueness of the western lamp was that the *Kohen*
always put into it half a *lug* of oil, the same amount of oil as
was put into each of the other six lamps (half a *lug* = 5 ½
oz.). This was sufficient to last for the longest nights of *Tevet*,
and yet it outburned all the candles.

They all burned the entire night and would extinguish in the early morning. In the summer, when the nights are shorter, they would burn into the morning hours. After they went out in the morning, the lamps would be cleaned out and fresh oil and new wicks would be placed in them. This service was known as *"hatavat haMenorah"* — "making good" — i.e. preparing the *Menorah* for kindling. The candles would not be lit again until the late afternoon. The western candle, however, continued burning the entire day until it was time to kindle the *Menorah* again in the evening.

*   *   *

This miraculous uninterrupted burning of the western lamp went on all the years of the first *Beit Hamikdash,* and served as a testimony for Hashem's presence in Israel. The western light continued to remain lit during the forty years that Shimon *HaTzaddik* was *Kohen Gadol* during the early years of the second *Beit Hamikdash.* Afterwards the Jewish people were not worthy of this miracle and sometimes the western candle would go out in the morning the same as did all the other six candles. To rekindle it in the evening, fire was taken from the Altar upon which burnt offerings were made.

(מס' יומא דף ל"ט ע"ב)

"יערך אתו אהרן מערב עד בקר לפני ה'"

**"Aaron shall arrange it, from evening
to morning, before Hashem." (24:3)**

QUESTION: Which one of the seven *Menorah* lamps was the western lamp, and how was it *"lifnei Hashem"* — "before Hashem"?

ANSWER: According to the opinion of Rabbi Elazer ben Rabbi Shimon that the lamps were from north to south, parallel to the *Parochet* which was on the west, all the candles were actually on the west side of the *Beit Hamikdash.* However, the wicks of the southern lamps pointed northward, toward the middle lamp of the *Menorah,* and the wicks of the three northern lamps pointed southward, toward the middle lamp of the *Menorah*. The wick of the middle lamp itself pointed westward towards the *Parochet* and Holy of Holies. Hence, it was considered *"lifnei Hashem"* — "before Hashem" — and designated as the *neir ma'aravi* — western lamp.

According to Rebbe, if the lamps were positioned from east to west, then presumably the westernmost lamp should have been the designated the "western lamp." Nevertheless, the western lamp is the second from the easternmost lamp for the following reason:

When the *Kohen* enters the *Beit Hamikdash*, he enters from the east and the first lamp he encounters is the easternmost. Obviously, since it is the most distant from the *lifnei Hashem* — before Hashem — i.e. the *Parochet* and Holy of Holies, it cannot be considered the western lamp which must be lit first. On the other hand, the *Kohen* could not pass up all the candles and start with the seventh lamp, which is westernmost, since we have a rule *"Ein mavirin al hamitzvot"* — "You may not pass over a *mitzvah*." Thus, it couldn't be that the Torah would want you to pass by all the lamps and not kindle them and go on to the end and then kindle the last one! Therefore, as a compromise, the second from the easternmost was designated as *neir ma'aravi* — "the western lamp." Hence, all requirements are met: it is to the west of the easternmost lamp and thus *"lifnei Hashem"* — "before Hashem" (the west). Moreover, we are not violating the rule of "not passing over" since it is the first one which the *Kohen* could light when he entered.

(מנחות דף צ״ח ע״ב)

״להעלות נר תמיד מחוץ לפרוכת העדות ...

יערוך אותו אהרן מערב עד בקר לפני ה׳ תמיד״

"To kindle a lamp continually. Outside of the *Parochet* of Testimony ... Aaron shall

arrange it, from evening to morning before
Hashem continually." (24:2,3)

QUESTION: Which candle did the *Kohen* light first?

ANSWER: The *Gemara* says of the western lamp that *"memeno hayah madlik ubo hayah mesaiyeim"* — "the *Kohen* would light from it and conclude with it." According *Rashi* the procedure was as follows:

In the evening the *Kohen* would remove the burning wick and hold it in his hand or place it in a dish. Then he would clean out the lamp, fill it with oil, and put in a new wick, which he then lit with the old wick.

After cleaning out and kindling the western candle, the *Kohen* would light the other candles from it. This was accomplished with the wicks of the candles, which were long enough to be pulled out and reach the wick in the adjoining lamp. Thus, the lamps on either side of the western lamp were kindled from the latter's wick, and these wicks kindled the lamp next in line, and so on.

Hence, according to *Rashi, "memeno hayah madlik"* means that after it was lit in the late afternoon, the others were then lit from it, and "concluding with it" refers to *hatavat haMenorah* — preparing the *Menorah*. The western candle was the last one to be prepared, since all the others were already prepared in the morning.

Tosafot is of the opinion that when the *Kohen* started the evening *Menorah* service, *"mimeno hayah madlik"* — he would first light the other candles from the old wick of the western candle. Then, when he started working on the western candle, it would extinguish, and he would put in fresh oil and a new wick and light it from the other candles. Hence, *"ubo hayah mesayeim"* means that the *hadlakah* — lighting — of the western candle was the conclusion of the daily *Menorah* kindling.

(רש״י ותוס׳ במס׳ שבת כ״ב ע״ב)

"בהעלתך את הנרת אל מול פני המנורה יאירו שבעת הנרות"

"When you kindle the lamps, toward the face of the Menorah shall the seven lamps light." (Bamidbar 8:2)

QUESTION: In what directions were the flames on the wicks pointing?

ANSWER: According to the opinion that the lamps were positioned from north to south (parallel to the *Parochet*), the three on the southern side of the main shaft — the middle lamp — were bending to north and the three on the northern side of the main shaft — middle lamp — were bending southward. And the light of the wick of the middle lamp tilted toward the Holy of Holies.

And according to the opinion that they were positioned from east to west (perpendicular to the *Parochet*), the three on the west were facing the middle, the three on the east were facing toward the middle lamp, and the wick of middle lamp pointed upward. Thus, according to both opinions, "to the face of the *Menorah*," meant the middle lamp.

A difficulty that begs explanation is that since all six lamps were facing to the middle one, it should have said "toward the face of the *Menorah* — the middle lamp — shall the *six* lamps light"?

An explanation given is that since the middle lamp did not turn to either side of the *Menorah* lamps, it might be said that it is facing to itself, and thus, together with the other six that are facing it, all the seven are facing "towards the face of the *Menorah*."

(עי' מנחות צ"ט ע"ב ובפי' הרא"ס ר"פ בהעלותך ובאנציקלופדי' תלמודית ח"ח ע' שי"ח)

There is yet another opinion that hold that all the wicks were tilted toward the *Shulchan* — Table — which stood in the north, opposite the *Menorah*. Thus, *all seven* were lighting *el mul penei HaMenorah* — to [the *Shulchan* which was on the] *opposite* side of the Menorah.

(רשב"ם עה"ת)

"שיטת הרמב"ם בהדלקת המנורה"
"The Rambam's opinion concerning *Menorah* lighting"

The Rambam has an entirely different approach in this matter. He holds that according to Rebbe who opines that the lamps were positioned from east to west, the *neir ma'aravi* — the western lamp — was the westernmost lamp. i.e. the lamp closest to the *Parochet* and Holy of Holies, and it was the first one to be lit.

In addition, the Rambam opines that according to Rebbe's opinion that the *Menorah* was positioned from east to west the flames on the wicks of *all* seven lamps were facing the west, towards the Holy of Holies. Thus, *"el mul penei haMenorah"* does not mean that the lights were facing the lamp on top of the central shaft, but that they were *all* facing the Holy of Holies which was *penei haMenorah — in front of* the *Menorah*.

Accordingly, this fits very well with the words "Towards the *penei haMenorah* shall the *seven* lamp lights illuminate (*Bamidbar* 8:2), since *all seven* lamps were facing to the direction (westward) which was *in front of* the *Menorah*, i.e. the Holy of Holies.

The Rambam is not concerned about the fact that when the *Kohen* enters and goes to the end of the *Menorah* to light it, he is passing over a *mitzvah*, since the Torah insisted *"lifnei Hashem"* — that the candle to be lit first should be the one which is closest to Hashem. Thus, the *mitzvah* is to kindle first the lamp most west, and the *mitzvah* to light the others commences only *after* this one is kindled.

(פי' המשניות להרמב"ם מס' תמיד ספ"ג ורפ"ו, ועי' אריכת הביאור ברשימת המנורה לכ"ק אדמו"ר)

* * *

Another novelty of the Rambam is his opinion that the *Menorah* was lit twice a day, in the evening and again in the morning. According to his view, we are commanded that all seven lights should burn continuously, day and night. Therefore, if the lamps are found still burning in the morning, they are attended to and allowed to continue burning. If they are found extinguished, they are cleaned out; that is, the wick and remaining oil are removed, the lamp is wiped clean, a new wick and new oil are put in, and the light is immediately lit; for Rambam (*Temidim U'musafim* 3:11) holds that *"hadlakat haneirot hi hatavatam"* — "The lighting of the lamps is what is called readying them," i.e., "lighting" and "readying" are the same act.

(פיה"מ תמיד ספ"ג, והל' תמידין ומוספין פ"ג הי"ב)

רעיונות על המנורה
Insights on the *Menorah*

"בהעלתך את הנרת"
"When you kindle the lamps...." (8:2)

QUESTION: Rashi writes that the *Kohen* stood on a step *"u'meitiv"* — cleaned out the ashes and prepared wicks and oil for the kindling of the *Menorah*. Why doesn't he say *"u'madlik"* — "and kindled"?

ANSWER: According to *halachah*, *"Hadlakah kesheirah bezar"* — "even a non-*Kohen*, may kindle the lamps, if the *Menorah* was brought outside" (Rambam, *Be'at Hamikdash* 9:7). However, preparing the wicks of the *Menorah* must be performed only by a *Kohen*. Thus, Rashi uses the expression *"meitiv"* — "prepared" — without saying that the *Kohen* kindled the lamps.

(ר' אברהם מרדכי זצ"ל מגור)

*   *   *

King Shlomo says, "The soul of man is a candle of G-d (Proverbs 20:27). Every Jew must see to it that his candle shines brightly and also assure that another Jew's candle is lit. This is accomplished by studying Torah, doing *mitzvot,* and inspiring others to do likewise.

"Hadlakah kesheirah bezar" — every Jew must kindle the flame of his *neshamah* as well as the *neshamah* of another Jew but only a *"Kohen"* — a true Jewish leader — is qualified to do *"hatavah"* — determine the authentic path of the Torah.

(לקוטי שיחות ח"ב ע' 317)

"וזה מעשה המנורה מקשה זהב"

"And this is the workmanship of the *Menorah*, beaten out gold." (8:3)

QUESTION: Rashi writes that Moshe had difficulty understanding the making of the *Menorah*. What couldn't Moshe comprehend about the *Menorah*?

ANSWER: One of the esoteric interpretations of the *Menorah* is that it symbolized *Klal Yisrael*. (See *Likkutei Torah, Beha'alotecha*.)

The *Menorah* was kindled with pure olive oil. According to the *Gemara* (*Menachot* 85b) olive oil is associated with knowledge.

Throughout the long exile, the Jewish people were scattered to all corners of the world. Wherever they sojourned, the country benefited immensely from their wisdom, intellect, and creativity. Nevertheless, anti-Semitism usually prevailed, and the Jewish people, who enhanced the country, were beaten and persecuted.

This strange phenomenon puzzled Moshe. The Jewish people, who have contributed so much to humanity through their intellect and wisdom, should be cherished and appreciated by all. Instead they were being persecuted!?

(מצאתי בכתבי אבי הרב שמואל פסח ז"ל באגאמילסקי)

"וזה מעשה המנרה מקשה זהב"

"And this is the workmanship of the *Menorah*, hammered out gold." (8:4)

QUESTION: Regarding the *Chatzotrot* — two trumpets — which were used to gather together *K'lal Yisrael* or the princes of the tribes, the Torah prescribed that "*Mikshah ta'aseh otom*" — "make them hammered out" (*Bamidbar* 10:2). Of the *Cheruvim* placed on top of the Ark, the Torah instructs "*Mikshah ta'aseh otom*" — "hammered out shall you make them" (*Shemot* 25:18).

Why were the trumpets, the *cheruvim* on top of the Ark (*Shemot* 25:18), and the *Menorah* all made "*mikshah*" — hammered out?

ANSWER: The word "*mikshah*" (מקשה) stems from the word "*kashah*" (קשה) — "difficult." Hammering something out from a piece of metal is quite difficult and laborious.

The *Cheruvim* were images of children (see *Shemot* 25:18, Rashi). The *Menorah* represents Torah and *mitzvot*, as stated: "For a *mitzvah* is a lamp and Torah is light" (Proverbs 6:23). The trumpets were used to gather together and unite *K'lal Yisrael* or the princes of the tribes.

Raising children successfully, progressing in Torah, and assuring that one's children remain attached and focused on the Ark — Torah — is not easily achieved. To unite *K'lal Yisrael* or the princes of the tribes is not an easy task. To learn Torah, observe *mitzvot*, and live an authentic Torah lifestyle requires much effort and dedication. Each one of the three is "*kashah*" — "difficult" — and each requires "*mikshah*" — "hammering" — much laborious effort.

(שמעתי מר׳ אהרן מרדכי שי׳ (ארטור) לוקסטענבערג)

"כמראה אשר הראה ה׳ את משה כן עשה את המנורה"

"According the image that Hashem showed Moshe, so did he make the *Menorah*." (8:4)

QUESTION: Rashi (*Shemot* 25:40) writes that "Moshe was perplexed by the construction of the *Menorah* until Hashem showed him a *Menorah* of fire." Why was it so difficult for Moshe to comprehend the making of the *Menorah?*

ANSWER: Regarding "*Binah*" — "understanding" — the *Gemara* (*Rosh Hashanah* 21b) says that "Fifty gates of understanding were created in the world; all but one, were given to Moshe."

The *Menorah* represents Torah wisdom, as the *Gemara* (*Bava Batra* 25b) says, "One who wishes to become knowledgeable should face south during his prayers. The way to remember this rule is that the *Menorah* is on the south side." With its lights it is symbolic of Torah knowledge, as King Shlomo says in Proverbs (6:23), "For the *mitzvah* is a candle, and the Torah is light." (*Rabbeinu Gershon*, ibid.)

On the *Menorah* there were seven branches, eleven knobs, nine flowers and twenty two goblets — a total of forty nine items, corresponding to the 49 gates of understanding. The central shaft of the *Menorah*, from which everything projected, corresponded to the fiftieth gate of understanding.

Since the *Menorah* represents the fifty gates of understanding and Moshe attained only 49, it was difficult for him to comprehend the pattern of the *Menorah* until Hashem showed him a fiery image of it.

(אדרת אליהו פ׳ דברים)

"וראה ועשה כתבניתם אשר אתה מראה בהר"

"See and construct, according to their form that you are shown on the mountain."
(*Shemot* 25:40)

QUESTION: How did Hashem relieve Moshe's difficulty in comprehending the construction of the *Menorah* by telling him that he should construct it according to the form he was shown on the mountain?

ANSWER: Moshe's difficulty stemmed from the fact that the *Menorah* represented the 50 gates of wisdom and he only attained 49 (see above). According to the *Arizal* (*Likkutei Torah, Va'etchanan*) when Moshe was on the mountain with Hashem he achieved the comprehension of all the 50 gates of wisdom. Moshe retained this exalted state up to the time when the Jews sinned with the golden calf. At that time Moshe was together with Hashem on the mountain, and Hashem said to him *"Leich, reid"* (לך רד) — "Go, descend [for your nation that you have brought up from Egypt has degenerated *Shemot* 32:7]. Rashi writes that Hashem told

Moshe *"Reid migdulatecha"* — "Descend from your greatness."
The word *"leich"* (לך) — has the numerical value of 50.
Hashem told Moshe, "Now that your people have
degenerated, descend from your greatness. Until now you
achieved comprehension of all 50 gates of wisdom and from
now on, *reid* — go down — from *leich* — the 50 gates you
formerly achieved and you will now only have 49."

Moshe conveyed to the people Hashem's command
concerning the construction of the Tabernacle and its vessels
on the day after *Yom Kippur,* which was some three months
after they sinned with the golden calf. At this time he no
longer had the knowledge of the fiftieth gate of wisdom and
therefore experienced difficulty in comprehending the
concept of *Menorah.*

Hence, Hashem said to Moshe, "You already were shown
it on the mountain and at that time you comprehended it
very well since you had reached the 50th gate. Therefore,
though you are currently lacking comprehension of the 50th
gate you should be able to construct it."

(הרב פנחס שי׳ פרידמן, מחנה חרדי)

* * *

Incidentally, this fits very well into the terminology used
in the *Gemara.* "There are 50 gates of wisdom and *'kulam nitnu
l'Moshe chaseir achat'* — 'they were all given to Moshe, less
one." It does not say that he was given only 49 of the 50,
rather, *"kulam nitnu l'Moshe"* — *all* of them i.e. the entire 50
were given to Moshe, "less one" — although one was taken
back from him afterward when the Jews sinned with the
golden calf.

שמן — Oil

"ואתה תצוה את בני ישראל ויקחו אליך שמן זית זך
כתית למאור להעלת נר תמיד"

**"And you shall command the Children of Israel,
that they shall take for you pure olive oil,
crushed for illumination, to kindle a lamp
continually." (Shemot 27:20)**

QUESTION: What message does Moshe's command concerning oil for the *Menorah* convey to the Jewish people for posterity?

ANSWER: *"Veyikchu eilecha shemen zayit zach"* — "They shall take for you pure olive oil." Olive oil does not mix with any other liquid, but rather separates and rises to the top. This reminds the Jews that they are unique, and should not mix and assimilate with others.

"Katit lama'or" — "Crushed for illumination." The *"ma'or"* represents the light of Torah: as stated in Proverbs (6:23), "Torah is *or* — light." In order to truly succeed in Torah study, one needs to "crush" oneself, as our Sages tell us, *"Yagati umatzati ta'amin"* — "If someone says, 'I have toiled and I have succeeded' believe him" (*Megillah* 6b).

"Leha'alot neir tamid" — "to kindle a lamp continually." The "lamp" represents the soul of the Jew — *"Neir Hashem nishmat adam"* — "The 'lamp' of Hashem is the soul of the person" (Proverbs 20:27). The purpose of the Jew in this world is *"leha'alot neir tamid"* — to continually elevate his soul.

(משכנותיך ישראל)

"שמן זית זך כתית למאור"

"Pure olive oil, crushed for illumination."
(27:20)

QUESTION: The *Gemara* (*Menachot* 86a) says that the olives were divided into three grades, superior, intermediate and inferior. The oil of each grade was divided into three quality levels. The first level of the superior grade was supreme, and it was used for the kindling of the *Menorah*. The second oil of the superior grade and the first oil of the intermediate grade were equally acceptable for *menachot* — meal-offerings — but only the first oil of the intermediate grade could be used for the *Menorah*, and not the second oil of the superior grade. The third oil of the superior grade and the second oil of the intermediate grade and the first oil of the inferior grade were all equal for *menachot*, but only the first oil of the inferior grade could be used for the *Menorah*.

Why should the first oil of the inferior grade have priority for the kindling of the *Menorah* over the second and third oil of the superior grade?

ANSWER: Not all men are alike. Some have better faculties and some poorer. King Shlomo says, *"Neir Hashem nishmat adam"* — "A man's soul is the candle of G-d" (Proverbs 20:27) — and all the details connected with the *Menorah* contain teachings which apply to man's life. The lesson that can be learned from the law concerning the different levels of oil is that Hashem does not expect one person to be like another person, but He does expect him to achieve *his* utmost. Therefore, if one is capable of being on the highest level, one may not settle for being second. On the other hand, if one is only capable of the second level and one excels in that, his achievement equals that of the one who is uppermost in the first level.

*   *   *

The famous *tzaddik* Rabbi Zusha of Anipoli once said, "When I come before the Heavenly tribunal, I am not afraid that they will demand of me, 'Why wasn't Zusha like the patriarch Avraham?' Because I will reply, "I am not Avraham." But I am afraid lest they ask me, 'Why wasn't Zusha as Zusha could have been?'"

Likewise, a parent or teacher should never say to a child or student "why didn't you do on your exam as good as the other child did," rather they should demand "why didn't you do as good as *you* are capable of doing."

(שמעתי מדיין יצחק דוב שי' בערגער מלאנדאן, אנגלי')

"שמן זית זך כתית למאור"

"Pure olive oil, crushed for illumination."
(27:20)

QUESTION: Rashi explains that the first drop of oil which was extracted when crushed in a mortar is the finest, and such oil was used to kindle the *Menorah*. The remaining oil of the olive which was extracted by grinding the olives in a mill, was not as pure, and was used for *menachot* — meal offerings.

Normally, one uses the best oil for baking and cheaper oil for burning or lighting. Why in the *Mishkan* was it the reverse?

ANSWER: The *Menorah* is the prototype of spirituality. It represents Torah and *mitzvot,* as King Shlomo states, *"Neir mitzvah veTorah or"* — "A candle is a *mitzvah* and Torah is light" (Proverbs 6:23). A *Karban Minchah* is eaten and represents the material and physical needs of a person.

Unfortunately, there are people who plead poverty when they have to spend money for Torah and *mitzvot,* but have plenty of money when it comes to personal matters. From the way things were done in the *Mishkan,* we can learn true priorities. For Torah and *mitzvot* one should spend money and use the best and purest. For personal pleasure, a Jew should practice restraint and learn to suffice with less.

(כלי יקר)

"ויקחו אליך שמן זית זך"

"They shall take for you pure olive oil." (27:20)

QUESTION: Why does the Torah use the word *"zayit"* (olive) in the singular, rather than *"zeitim"* (plural)?

ANSWER: When food the size of an egg or larger becomes *tamei* (defiled), it can transmit defilement to other liquids. In smaller amounts, it can become *tamei*, but cannot transmit its *tumah* (defilement).

The oil in the olive is considered as though it is enclosed in a casing within the olive. Consequently, even when an olive becomes *tamei*, the oil in it retains its purity.

Although the oil is considered a *separate entity* within the olive, it is measured together with the olive for purposes of transmitting *tumah*. Thus, if the size of the *tamei* olive is bigger than an egg, the first drop of oil pressed becomes *tamei* as soon as it touches the outside skin (see *Pesachim* 33b).

When Moshe instructed the Jews to contribute olives in order to make pure oil for the *Menorah*, a problem arose. The olives in their possession were brought with them from Egypt. They were unsure about their purity and in doubt whether they could be used for the *Mishkan*.

Moshe therefore advised them to use average-sized olives, normally equal to half an egg. He also told them *not* to squeeze more than one olive at a time. Consequently, even if the olive was defiled, it would not be large enough to transmit *tumah* to the oil that came out.

(פנים יפות)

"ויקחו אליך שמן זית זך כתית למאור להעלת נר תמיד"

"They should take for you pure olive oil, crushed for illumination, to kindle a lamp continually." (27:20)

QUESTION: Would it not have been sufficient to just say, "They should take for you pure olive oil for the light." Why are the words *"katit"* — crushed — and *"leha'alot neir tamid"* — to kindle a lamp continually needed?

ANSWER: The first *Beit Hamikdash* existed for 410 years, and the second lasted 420 years. During the entire 830 years the *Menorah* was kindled every day. We all hope to merit speedily the third *Beit Hamikdash*, which will last forever. The elaboration in the *pasuk* is a *remez* — hint — to this.

The word *"katit"* (כתית) — "crushed" — has in it the letters ״כ״and ״ת״, whose numerical value is 420, and the letters ״י״ and ״ת״, which has a numerical value of 410. The oil should be ״כתית״ — for 830 years of lighting the *Menorah*. Afterwards, will be *"leha'alot neir tamid"* — the third *Beit Hamikdash* — in which the candles will be lit forever.

(בעל הטורים - תולדות יצחק)

Megilat Antiochus
The Scroll
of the Hasmoneans

Megilat Hachasmona'im, known also as *Megilat Antiochus,* has come down to us in both Aramaic and Hebrew. The Hebrew version (see *Siddur Otzer Yisrael*) is a literal translation from the Aramaic original, which was composed probably in the seventh century and published for the first time in Montoba in 1557. During the Middle Ages this *Megillah* was read in the Italian synagogues on *Chanukah* just as the Book of Esther is read on *Purim.* It still forms part of the liturgy of the Yemenite Jews. Saadyah *Gaon* attributed its authorship to the five sons of Matityahu.

Per translation by Phillip Birnbaum, 1974
with some modifications.

THE SCROLL OF THE HASMONEANS

The Greek monarch Antiochus was a powerful ruler; all the kings heeded him. He subdued many provinces and mighty sovereigns; he destroyed their castles, burned their palaces and imprisoned their men. Since the reign of Alexander there had never been a king like him beyond the Euphrates. He erected a large city on the seacoast to serve as his royal residence, and called it "Antioch" after his own name. Opposite it his governor Bagris founded another city, and called it "City of Bagris" after himself. Such are their names to this day.

In the twenty-third year of his reign, the two hundred and thirteenth year after the Temple had been rebuilt, Antiochus determined to march on Jerusalem. He said to his officers: "You are aware that the Jews of Jerusalem are in our midst. They neither offer sacrifices to our gods nor observe our laws; they abandon the king's laws to practice their own. They hope moreover for the day when kings and tyrants shall be crushed, saying: 'O that our own king might reign over us, that we might rule the sea and the land, so that the entire world would be ours.' It is indeed a disgrace for the royal government to let them remain on the face of the earth. Come now, let us attack them and abolish the covenant made with them: *Shabbat, Rosh Chodesh* and circumcision." The proposal pleased his officers and all his host.

Immediately king Antiochus dispatched his governor Nicanor with a large body of troops. He came to the Jewish, city of Jerusalem and massacred many people; he set up a heathen altar in the Temple, concerning which the G-d of Israel had said to his faithful prophets: "There will I establish my residence forever." In that very place they slaughtered a swine and brought its blood into the holy court. When Yochanan ben Matityahu heard of this deed, he was filled with rage and his face changed color. In his heart he drew a plan of action. He then made himself a dagger, two spans

long and one span wide, and concealed it under his clothes.
He came to Jerusalem and stood at the royal gate, calling to
this gate-keepers: "I am Yochanan ben Matityahu; I have
come to appear before Nicanor." The guards informed
Nicanor that the high priest of the Jews was standing at the
door. "Let him enter!" Nicanor said.

Yochanan was admitted to Nicanor, who said: "You are
one of the rebels who-rebel against the king and do not care
for the welfare of his government!" Yochanan replied: "My
lord, I have come to you; whatever you demand I will do." "If
you wish to do as I please," said Nicanor, "then take a swine
and sacrifice it upon the altar. You shall wear royal clothes
and ride the king's own horse; you shall be counted among
the king's close friends." To this, Yochanan answered: "My
lord, I am afraid of the Israelites; if they hear that I have done
such a thing they will stone me. Let everyone leave your
presence, so as not to inform them." Immediately Nicanor
ordered everybody out.

At, that moment Yochanan ben Matityahu raised his eyes
to heaven and prayed; "My G-d and G-d of my fathers
Avraham, Yitzchak, and Yaakov, do not hand me over to this
heathen; for if he kills me, he will boast in the temple of
Dagon that his god has handed me over to him." He
advanced three steps toward Nicanor, thrust the dagger into
his heart, and flung him fatally wounded into the court of the
Temple. "My G-d," Yochanan prayed, "do not count it a sin
that I killed this heathen in the Sanctuary; punish thus all the
foes who came with him to persecute Judea and Jerusalem."
On that day Yochanan set out and fought the enemy,
inflicting heavy slaughter on them. The number of those who
were slain by him on that day totaled two thousand seven
hundred. Upon returning, he erected a column with the
inscription: "Maccabee, Destroyer of Tyrants."

When king Antiochus heard that his governor Nicanor
had been slain, he was bitterly distressed. He sent for wicked
Bagris, the deceiver of his people, and told him: "Do you not

know, have you not heard, what the Israelites did to me? They massacred my troops and ransacked my camps! Can you now be sure of your wealth? Will your homes remain yours? Come, let us move against them and abolish the covenant which their G-d made with them: *Shabbat, Rosh Chodesh,* and circumcision." Then wicked Bagris and his hosts invaded Jerusalem, murdering the population and proclaiming an absolute decree against *Shabbat, Rosh Chodesh,* and circumcision. So drastic was the king's edict that when a man was discovered to have circumcised his son, he and his wife were hanged along with the child. A woman gave birth to a son after her husband's death and had him circumcised when he was eight days old. With the child in her arms, she went up on top of the wall of Jerusalem and cried out: "We say to you, wicked Bagris: This covenant of our fathers which you intend to destroy shall never cease from us nor from our children's children." She cast her son down to the ground and flung herself after him so that they died together. Many Israelites of that period did the same, refusing to renounce the covenant of their fathers.

Some of the Jews said to one another: "Come, let us keep *Shabbat* in a cave lest we violate it." When they were betrayed to Bagris, he dispatched armed men who sat down at the entrance of the cave and said: "You Jews, surrender to us! Eat of our bread, drink of our wine, and do what we do!" But the Jews said to one another: "We remember what we were commanded on Mount Sinai: 'Six days you shall labor and do all your work; on the seventh day you shall rest.' It is better for us to die than to desecrate *Shabbat.*" When the Jews failed to come out, wood was brought and set on fire at the entrance of the cave. About a thousand men and women died there. Later the five sons of Matityahu, Yochanan and his four brothers, set out and routed the hostile forces, whom they drove to the coast; for they trusted in the G-d of heaven.

Wicked Bagris, accompanied by those who had escaped the sword, boarded a ship and fled to king Antiochus. "O king," he said, "you have issued a decree abolishing *Shabbat, Rosh Chodesh,* and circumcision in Judea, and now there is complete rebellion there. The five sons of Matityahu cannot be defeated unless they are attacked by all the combined forces; they are stronger than lions, swifter than eagles, braver than bears. Be pleased to accept my advice, and do not fight them with this small army lest you be disgraced in the sight of all the kings. Send letters to all your royal provinces; let all the army officers without exception come with armored elephants." This pleased king Antiochus. He sent letters to all his royal domains, and the chieftains of various clans arrived with armored elephants. Wicked Bagris invaded Jerusalem for the second time. He broke through the wall, shattered the gateway, made thirteen breaches in the Temple, and ground the stones to dust. He thought to himself: "This time they shall not defeat me; my army is numerous, my hand is mighty." However, the G-d of heaven did not think so.

The five sons of Matityahu went to Mizpeh in Gilead, where the house of Israel had been saved in the days of Shmuel *Hanavi.* They fasted, sat in ashes and prayed to the G-d of heaven for mercy; then a good plan came to their mind. These were their names: Yehudah, the firstborn; Shimon, the second; Yochanan, the third; Yonatan, the fourth; Elazar, the fifth. Their father blessed them, saying: "Yehudah my son, I compare you to Yehudah the son of Yaakov who was likened to a lion. Shimon my son, I compare, you to Shimon the son of Yaakov who slew the men of Shchem. Yochanan my son, I compare you to Avner the son of Ner, general of Israel's army. Yonatan my son, I compare you to Yonatan the son of Shaul who defeated the Philistines. Elazar my son, I compare you to Pinchas the son of Elazar, who was zealous for his G-d and rescued the Israelites." Soon afterwards the five sons of Matityahu attacked the pagan forces, inflicting severe losses upon them. One, of the brothers, Yehudah, was killed.

When the sons of Matityahu discovered that Yehudah had been slain, they returned to their father who asked: "Why did you come back?" They replied: "Our brother Yehudah, who alone equaled all of us, has been killed." "I will join you in the battle against the heathen," Matityahu said, "lest they destroy the house of Israel; why be so dismayed over your brother?" He joined his sons that same day and waged war against the enemy. The G-d of heaven delivered into their hands all swordsmen and archers, army officers and high officials. None of these survived. Others were compelled to seek refuge in the coastal cities. In attacking the elephants, Elazar was engulfed in their dung. His brothers searched for him among the living and the dead, and could not find him. Eventually, however, they did find him.

The Jews rejoiced over the defeat of their enemies, some of whom were burned while others, were hanged on the gallows. Wicked Bagris was included among those who were burned to death. When king Antiochus heard that his governor Bagris and the army officers had been killed, he boarded a ship and fled to the coastal cities. Wherever he came the people rebelled and called him "The Fugitive," so he drowned himself in the sea.

The Hasmoneans entered the Sanctuary, rebuilt the gates, closed the breaches, and cleansed the Temple court from the slain and the impurities. They looked for pure olive oil to light the *Menorah,* and found only one bottle with the seal of the *Kohen Gadol* so that they were sure of its purity. Though its quantity seemed sufficient only for one day's lighting, it lasted for eight days owing to the blessing of the G-d of heaven who had established His Name there. Hence, the Hasmoneans and all the Jews alike instituted these eight days as a time of feasting and rejoicing, like any festival prescribed in the Torah, and of kindling lights to commemorate the victories G-d had given them. Mourning and fasting are forbidden on *Chanukah,* except in the case of an individual's vow which must be discharged. Nevertheless, the Hasmoneans did not prohibit work on this holiday.

From that time on the Greek government was stripped of its renown. The Hasmoneans and their descendants ruled for two hundred and six years, until the destruction of the *Beit Hamikdash*.

And so the Jews everywhere observe this festival for eight days, beginning on the twenty-fifth of *Kislev*. These days, instituted by *Kohanim*, Levites and Sages of Temple times, shall be celebrated by their descendants forever.

* * *

The Al-mighty Who performed for them a miracle and wonder, may He perform for us miracles and wonders. And we should see the fulfillment of what is written (Michah 7:15) "As in the days when you left the land of Egypt I will show it wonders."

לזכות

כ"ק אדוננו מורנו ורבנו

אור עולם

נזר ישראל ותפארתו

צדקת ד' עשה

ומשפטיו עם ישראל

ורבים השיב מעון

הגאון האלקי מרנא ורבנא

מנחם מענדל

בן הרב הגאון החסיד המקובל רבי **לוי יצחק** נ"ע

עלה השמימה מוצש"ק שלישי לחודש תמוז
שנת ה' **תהא שנת** נפלאות דגולות
ליצירה